Dear Solomon,
My Finances are a Mess

To my partners
in the ministry,
Terry & Barb

[signature]

Prov. 27:23-24

DEAR SOLOMON, MY FINANCES ARE A MESS

Al Smith

ELM HILL

A Division of
HarperCollins Christian Publishing

www.elmhillbooks.com

Published in Nashville, Tennessee, by Elm Hill, an imprint of Thomas Nelson. Elm Hill and Thomas Nelson are registered trademarks of HarperCollins Christian Publishing, Inc.

Elm Hill titles may be purchased in bulk for educational, business, fund-raising, or sales promotional use. For information, please e-mail SpecialMarkets@ ThomasNelson.com.

All Scripture quotations, unless otherwise indicated, are taken from the New American Standard Bible'. Copyright © 1960, 1962, 1963, 1968, 1971, 1972, 1973, 1975, 1977, 1995 by The Lockman Foundation. Used by permission. (www.Lockman.org)

Library of Congress Cataloging-in-Publication Data

Library of Congress Control Number: 2019907161

ISBN 978-1-400326471 (Paperback)
ISBN 978-1-400326488 (eBook)

DEDICATION

This book would have never been written or published apart from the encouragement and undying support of my wife, Connie. God's gracious provision of such a treasure has been and continues to be the very definition of the "helpmate" described when the Almighty created Eve for Adam. She has been a living example of many of the principles detailed in this book, long before God convinced me of their value. Thank you, my love.

CONTENTS

Introduction

I can recall the excitement and the anticipation. It was Easter and Dad was hiding the eggs for my brother and me while we fidgeted in the bedroom, baskets in hand, behind closed doors. My brother was three years younger, so I was told to leave the eggs that were out in the open for him to find, but I didn't always follow those instructions very well; after all, no self-respecting kid could let his little brother find more eggs than he did. There were eggs on the coffee table, eggs on the plastic-covered couch and chairs, eggs on the television set—all in plain view for anyone who was even half-heartedly looking. But there were also eggs hidden behind pillows, underneath the couch and chairs, and mixed in with the bowl full of wax fruit that was proudly displayed on the aforementioned coffee table; but even those eggs were simple to discover for those who were intent on finding them.

Finding Easter eggs was not a difficult task because my dad made it easy on us; he wanted us to find them. One reason he probably wanted us to find them was because, one particular Easter, we didn't find one until the odor became very apparent many weeks after the fact; but, primarily, he wanted us to find them because of the smiles on our faces. He delighted in our joy.

God delights in the joy of His children. Our Heavenly Father has something far more beneficial for His children to find than multicolored, hard-boiled eggs. God is delighted when we find His wisdom. Like the eggs, His wisdom is easy to find for those who are looking. Unlike the eggs, His wisdom is actually calling out to us, literally shouting to us so there is no doubt in where to look. Yet, so many wander and stumble and feel their way through this life as if they were commanded to look for wisdom while blindfolded.

"Wisdom shouts in the street, she lifts her voice in the square; at the head of the noisy *streets* she cries out; at the entrance of the gates in the city she utters her sayings" (Proverbs 1:20-21 NASB).

During my childhood, one of the more popular newspaper columns was called "Dear Abby." It was an advice column. People would send in their letters detailing their personal problems and Abby would dispense advice for all of America to read. The popularity of advice columns in newspapers has waned over the years, but Abby—and later, Ann Landers (her twin sister)—developed quite a following in their day. And while the advice they dished out was generally just plain common sense, it was lacking in genuine authority. Abby and Ann were just a couple of country girls who had a gift for seeing the obvious.

Solomon has the authority that Abby and Ann were missing. Solomon was the wisest man who ever set foot on this earth. And God has declared that never again will a man have the same level of wisdom that Solomon was blessed with. Solomon never solicited letters of those who were seeking advice, but he did write the epitome of all advice columns during his day. The Book of Proverbs contains words to live by and answers to many of life's questions.

Proverbs contains advice on relationships with your spouse, your children, your parents, your employers, your employees, your friends, your enemies, the authorities in your life, and just about any other human relationship you could imagine. There is advice on how to handle your finances; how to deal with life and with death; how to use the power of your tongue; how to influence people; how to pray; how to live righteously; how to avoid sin; and how to identify and interact with foolish people, stubborn people, wicked people, and dangerous people.

You will find advice on greediness, good health and well-being, learning, human nature, honor, humility, love, hatred, deceitfulness, morality and immorality, proper planning, pride, priorities, service, testing, and listening.

Solomon has wisdom for growing old, handling authority, obedience, raising children, discipline, marriage, understanding, integrity, borrowing and lending, wealth and prosperity, work, benevolence, friendship, neighbors, government, and keeping a good reputation.

You may have to dig, and you may not have a specific answer to your particular problem, but, if you are genuinely searching, you will find a principle in the Book of Proverbs that will help you in a lasting and meaningful way.

We all need advice from time to time—even Solomon, apparently, needed some help because a few of his wise friends contributed to the writing of Proverbs—but we need advice from someone with authority. We need advice from someone who has our best interests at heart. We need true wisdom to deal with the issues we face in today's world.

It's yours for the taking. It's in plain view and it's calling your name.

* * *

For many years, God has given me a ministry of writing devotional thoughts in the form of what was once a daily email. I spent many years working my way through this glorious book of Proverbs. I have leaned on several who have blazed the trail ahead of me in commenting on this book, but have primarily leaned on the Holy Spirit to give me personal and practical illustrations to help illuminate the truth of this immensely practical book of the Bible.

As I began to formulate ideas for how to best communicate the wisdom of Proverbs to those who are searching for God's wisdom, the Holy Spirit led me to start categorizing the Proverbs. It wasn't long after when the Spirit impressed upon me the idea of a divine advice column of sorts; and hence "Dear Solomon" was born with this first installment on finances and possessions.

To a certain degree, I always struggle writing devotions on the topic of handling money and possessions. I know and understand the biblical principles, but I have been a poor example in being obedient to God's wisdom on this topic in my own life until recently. For the most part, I have done things my own way in the aspects of finance and material possessions. I have always been a cheerful and generous giver when it came to tithes and offerings, but, after that, it has been pretty much a hit-and-miss proposition when it comes to following God's principles of finance.

God had been gently nudging me in the right direction as I worked through writing a devotional thought on each and every Proverb, which obviously included a generous portion that dealt with money and possessions. But when I reached the end of chapter 27, the gentle nudge turned into a cold slap—"**Know well the condition of your flocks, *and* pay attention to your herds; for riches are not forever, nor does a crown endure to all generations**" (27:23-24).

This Proverb was like a hammer and I was the proverbial nail, so forgive me if I ramble on a bit about my own issues. For most of my adult life, I flew by the seat of my pants when it came to handling the money God had entrusted to my care. Borrowing money and using credit cards was simply a way of life. I fell for the philosophy of *"If I could afford the monthly payments, I could afford to make the purchase."* The problem with this philosophy, besides being against God's principles, is that you have to presume that you will always have a job and that that job will always provide enough income to keep up with the obligations you are committed to.

God has always been merciful, and He has taken my wife and me through some tough times over the years, but we learned the lesson of presumption when, six months into a new house and a new mortgage, my wife was laid off—and she was the major breadwinner at the time.

The principles God hammered into my rather thick noggin are to pay attention to the money God gives me and don't presume that the future will always be bright while we dwell in these earthly tents. Don't just stand idly by while the markets are going into the tank. Be wise in your investments. Adjust as conditions change. **"Know well the condition of your flocks, and pay attention to your herds."** And while many may have been a little lax in heeding the advice of God in this Proverb, all should now understand that **riches are not forever**.

Do you want to know the real kicker in my lack of following God's principles in handling my money? At the time God was making sure I understood this simple yet profound thought, I was a bivocational pastor. My job outside of the church was insurance and financial planning—and I was good at it with other people's money! I told my clients to get out of the market in June of 2008. Those who listened are still in pretty good shape today. Those who didn't lost a ton. So, how in the world can I be so apt to follow God's principles when handling other people's money but so inept when I am handling my own?

The answer is in the wording of the question—I consider the money and possessions I have to be my own instead of understanding that they belong to God. I was good with my client's money because I understood that I was a steward who was expected to take extreme care in preserving and growing their investment. Because I have viewed the money I have as my own and not as money that I am a steward of for God, I have been careless.

As I said earlier, that view with me has changed. So, whether you have been like me in how you have handled the money and possessions God has entrusted to your care, or this is just a confirmation that you are on the right track, may the Lord use this Proverb and my life's example to help you from this point onward.

I trust you will be as blessed as I have been by this fascinating journey God has allowed me to be a part of. But, just like the eggs I searched for as a child, the wisdom of God is only for those who are genuinely searching; but if you do find yourself among the privileged few who put forth the effort, you will fill your basket to overflowing. So, open the bedroom door of your heart and let the excitement of the hunt begin!

CHAPTER 1

CAN'T GET ENOUGH

There are plenty of things in my life that I have overindulged in. There has hardly been a dessert that I have met that survived the meeting; I have yet to grow weary of watching sports on TV; and I consistently run out of room on my bookshelves no matter how many I have in the house or at my office. I guess there are worse things to never be able to get enough of, but these are not good examples of what truly matters. My waistline and health suffer when I eat too many desserts; there are better uses of my time than sitting in front of the TV; and, while worthy books can be put to very good use, I have far too many on my shelves that have never been opened, potentially leaving answers I have been looking for within arm's reach.

There are other things that you could never overindulge in or have too much of. All of us have room for more love in our life. I have never heard anyone say they are at their limit on good friends. We can never drink our fill of God's mercy. And wisdom is seemingly always in short supply, which is the issue I want to address in this opening chapter.

Apart from godly wisdom, we will never experience true satisfaction, independence, and contentment in our financial lives. So, before we start digging into the nuts and bolts of what Solomon has to say concerning money, possessions, work, etc., let's make sure we build a good foundation on the primary resource that must be accumulated and continually pursued in abundance.

I live in the central mountains of Colorado. When the weather begins to get colder and we experience the first few snowfalls of the season, the wildlife starts to make its way down to lower elevations in search of food. One of the more amazing animals that make their appearance at this time is the bighorn sheep. They prefer the steep, rocky cliffs as opposed to the open fields. You will see them on the edge of a cropping of rocks jutting out from the side of a sheer cliff and wonder how they got there. Then you watch them skillfully step or jump down then climb or leap up to another seemingly impossible perch of stone. They don't slip and they don't fall. Their steps are sure.

Listening your way to wisdom

Solomon makes a comparison between the wise and the foolish in Proverbs 10:8–9 using the illustration of being on firm ground or a slippery slope. Let's look at the foolish person first—"**a babbling fool will be ruined … he who perverts his ways will be found out.**"

The fool heads down a dangerous path. He doesn't take into consideration the obstacles in his way, or he doesn't care. A fool will only look at his current circumstances and the immediate need or desire. He does not want to hear advice, nor does he want to wait. He will use any means necessary to obtain what he wants even if it means using illegal or crooked means to do so. So, he goes headlong into whatever he is after without any regard for the pitfalls that lie ahead. Inevitably, he will fall and **be ruined**, as our Proverb says.

On the other hand, the wise person accepts instruction—"**The wise of heart will receive commands.**" Probably, the most important factor in obtaining wisdom is the willingness to be taught. Most lack this necessary quality. Most have too much pride in their life to accept the fact that they possibly do not know everything. Yet those who refuse instruction are counted as fools by God and people. It takes a man or woman of wisdom to seek instruction. It takes a man or woman of even greater wisdom to apply and follow instruction, which we will consider in a moment. Don't let pride keep you from asking for instruction when you lack knowledge or understanding, and then be diligent in applying wisdom. The fact that you are reading this book likely means you are on this path.

The wise also live a life of integrity—**"he who walks in integrity walks securely."** Maintaining honesty and integrity in your life at all times keeps you standing firmly no matter what your circumstances are. Just like the bighorn sheep, no matter how perilous your circumstances seem, you will not fall. The prophet Habakkuk says, **"The Lord GOD is my strength, and He has made my feet like hind's feet, and makes me walk on my high places"** (Habakkuk 3:19). This is what integrity will do for you; it will guide you safely through the mountains you face, including taming the money beast.

You must seek and accept knowledge to be equipped to transfer that knowledge into godly wisdom. So, how are you at heeding instructions? Do you follow them to the letter, or do you casually read or listen to them and then still do things your own way? The next Proverb we will look at implies that listening and adhering to instruction is a discipline that will endure—**"Cease listening, my son, to discipline, and you will stray from the words of knowledge"** (Proverbs 19:27).

In the first nine chapters of Proverbs, we are constantly encouraged to listen to and treasure the teaching that we receive. We are told that, in doing so, we are on the path to obtaining wisdom. This Proverb essentially says we are throwing all that wisdom out the door the minute we stop learning and the minute we refuse to accept instruction. At the point we think we know it all, wisdom is running for the exits.

I think the point is straightforward enough but let me give you an example of an area in which most Christians refuse instruction. It is an area of life that is bubbling over with opportunity to obtain wisdom, yet most ignore this opportunity and turn their backs on this knowledge. The area I speak of is in the trials and tribulations you face.

God allows trouble and pain and sorrow into our lives to teach us, to train us, to correct us, to mold us, to use us for His glory, and any number of other divine purposes. God is not sitting on a cloud watching and waiting for the perfect opportunity to make us miserable. We are all perfectly capable of and adept at making ourselves miserable without God's help. But each and every problem you face is a chance to increase in knowledge, and thus in wisdom. It is a time to grow and mature. It is a treasure chest brimming with golden nuggets of wisdom that cannot be obtained elsewhere.

If you can grasp this concept, if you can beat back your selfish desires that want nothing but pleasure and ease, if you can bring yourself to not only look for but see the silver lining in your dark clouds, then you will be able to begin to understand how James can tell us **"Consider it all joy, my brethren, when you encounter various trials"** (James 1:2). We will be able to consider our trials as an opportunity for great joy because we will understand the unspeakable opportunity that lies before us. We will know that the problems that lie at our feet are God's love being poured upon us. The Almighty Creator of the universe is taking the time to give you personalized instruction that is designed to make you wise and complete and mature in your life and in your faith, and He does so most effectively through personal difficulties.

But of course, God also gives you the freedom to turn your back on this instruction. He gives you the freedom to choose to worry and fret. He gives you the freedom to moan and complain. He allows you to make yourself sick and miserable. He even allows you to infect others with your negativity and hopelessness. Or, you can share your burdens with others, and open your eyes to the opportunity to learn all that the Master Teacher wants to invest into your life.

Now, even if it is your nature to be indecisive and negative, this is not a difficult choice. Listen to instruction, my child—in whatever form it presents itself.

I think it was Samuel Clemons (Mark Twain) who once borrowed from Proverbs and said something like this—*"Better to be thought a fool than to open your mouth and remove all doubt."* The point is, when you

are in the company of those who are wiser than you, don't try to ↓
them with your knowledge or attempt to play on their level; you are ↓
to only reveal your ignorance instead. You should rather humble yourse.
listen to what is being said, and, if you open your mouth at all, do so to
ask questions so that your understanding will be enhanced and increased.

Solomon shares two more Proverbs (10:13–14) with us, contrasting
the words of the wise with the words of the fool. Let's start this time by
looking at the wise person—**"On the lips of the discerning, wisdom is
found … Wise men store up knowledge."**

I have read several books on leadership over the years. One of the
common principles promoted in these books is to learn from those who
have already been successful in your field. One author spoke of being so
broke he couldn't put food on the table, yet he managed to scrape together
$100 for the privilege of spending fifteen minutes with a leader in his field.
Even though this author went hungry for a few days he said it was the best
investment he had ever made. The few nuggets of insight he gained in
that fifteen minutes propelled him to become a leader in that field not too
many years down the road.

What could you learn in fifteen minutes with the most successful person in your field? Better yet, what could you learn in fifteen minutes at
the feet of Jesus? This is what Mary (the sister of Martha and Lazarus) did
when Jesus came to visit. She sat at His feet and listened, soaking up every
drop of wisdom He imparted. Martha spent her time completing all of
the tasks of the day, tasks that would be there again tomorrow whether or
not they got done today. There is great wisdom in stopping and taking the
time to listen to those who have understanding.

The fool, on the other hand, only attracts trouble and punishment
when he opens his mouth—**"But a rod is for the back of him who lacks
understanding … with the mouth of the foolish, ruin is at hand."** Most
fools are afflicted with stubbornness. In his ignorance, a fool will continue
on in his foolishness even with the threat of punishment looming over
him. He's too stubborn to shut up or learn anything even when he has
seen the value of wisdom in action.

King Asa of Judah was like this. Early on in his reign he sought the Lord when the Egyptians were approaching to attack and the Lord defeated the Egyptian army. Later in his reign, Asa was again faced with an attacking army but, this time, it was Israel. Instead of inquiring of the Lord as he had in the past, he formed an alliance with Syria. Although the alliance worked from a military viewpoint and Israel was defeated, Asa's foolishness caused his kingdom to never have peace again during his reign. Later in his life, when Asa faced disease and sickness, he, again, did not seek God and the Lord allowed him to remain sick and disease-ridden all the way to his death.

Seeking godly wisdom is the same as seeking God through the reading, study, and application of His Word. We become fools when we ignore God and seek our answers apart from Him, and true wisdom will once again elude us.

Often, we refuse to seek instruction simply because we do not accept criticism of any kind. Criticism has been twisted by the devil to mean you are not being respected. R-E-S-P-E-C-T. Can you hear Aretha Franklin singing it? I think she was a little bit before her time; not that people didn't desire respect back in the '60s, but that generation had nothing on the people of today. People no longer simply desire to be respected, they demand it—and they will take your head off if you don't give it to them. The concept of *earning* respect is quickly becoming extinct.

Accepting criticism

Simmering beneath the surface in this issue is the fact that handling criticism, constructive or otherwise, is simply no longer accepted. If you criticize someone today, even in a lovingly constructive way, the recipient will more than likely take it as a sign of disrespect. Solomon speaks well to this issue—"**He whose ear listens to the life-giving reproof will dwell among the wise. He who neglects discipline despises himself, but he who listens to reproof acquires understanding**" (Proverbs 15:31–32).

I have been in church leadership in one form or another for the last forty years or so. Whenever a behavioral issue within the church has had to be handled, the guilty party rarely accepts being lovingly confronted and rightfully reproved for his or her sinful actions. They will, instead, take the words you say as a personal attack. You can be following Scripture to the letter in how you go about the process of confronting, and you can display the very love of Christ in doing so, yet most people will feel as if you are attacking them. They don't want to hear it—they reject what you have to say.

Our Proverb tells us this attitude is foolish and you are only hurting yourself when you react to criticism this way. Wisdom and understanding await those who accept constructive criticism, but far too many choose foolishness and self-inflicted harm instead. They would rather keep their dignity and self-respect (in their own eyes anyway) than to have their sin called out and corrected.

Here are two quick applications for us: First, don't automatically go on the defensive when someone is critical of your actions. They may be helping you correct a behavior in your life that is not biblical. Second, although it is not directly taught to us in this passage, understand that YOU are responsible to confront your brothers and sisters when they are sinning. Matthew 18:15–20 and Galatians 6:1–2 make this abundantly clear. Confront with the attitude of restoring their relationship with God and with man; confront with Christ's love in your heart; and confront with the attitude that you could just as easily be the one needing correction—but definitely confront when sin is revealed to you.

Whether or not criticism is involved, constructive or otherwise, it is a hard thing to even take advice from someone when you did not ask for it. When you are not looking for help, or you are not soliciting advice, or you don't even want to look at an instruction manual, you tend to ignore the advice that comes your way. Most of us can identify with this stubborn streak that runs through us (some to a greater measure than others), but most of us do not accept or believe the consequences of this folly. Our pride tells us that we know better than they do, and that you should not listen to someone else concerning your life. It truly is a difficult thing.

Loving criticism

Solomon addresses this struggle in another Proverb—**"Poverty and shame will come to him who neglects discipline, but he who regards reproof will be honored"** (Proverbs 13:18).

Solomon is clear that those who ignore or refuse to listen to the instruction and/or constructive criticism of others will see that their end will come to poverty and shame or disgrace. On the other hand, if you accept this instruction and/or constructive criticism in your lives, you will be honored. Solomon's choice of wording in that last phrase (**be honored**) could also be translated as "is made wealthy"—which fits as a true contrast to poverty just as honor contrasts shame.

Think back on the times in your life when you've wanted to kick yourself for not listening to the advice of others. Think about how you had that sickening feeling in the pit of your stomach when you realized that you had made a monumental mistake. I have known people who have lost multiplied thousands of dollars, and the respect of friends and family, because they chose to ignore the advice of others and do things their own way. I've also known folks who have profited greatly from following sound and godly advice.

In the modern-day remake of the movie *Sabrina*, the chauffeur had made millions over the course of his lifetime by listening to and acting upon the information he overheard his wealthy employers discussing in the back seat of the car. While this is obviously a fictional account, would the chauffeur have made those millions if he had ignored the information that was given? This fictional story helps make the point for us—advice and instruction that is ignored can lead us to a life of poverty and disgrace.

We all have been given the advice that we cannot wait until we are age sixty to start saving for retirement, but most Americans have waited that long, if they even start saving then. Choosing to live a larger lifestyle while we are young and ignoring the future will indeed bring poverty and shame later in life—just as heeding the advice that is available to us will bring honor and wealth.

Heeding advice

Leadership is a difficult pursuit. For some, the mantle of leadership is thrust upon them in a time of crisis and there is no looking back. For others, leadership is something they read about and study in hopes of one day becoming an effective leader. For others still, leadership is something they take by force, whether through military overthrow of a government or by playing the game of politics well. Regardless of how a person assumes a leadership role, they are in for a difficult responsibility—a responsibility that can be devastating instead of rewarding.

Solomon's next piece of wisdom is for everyone, but it has particular application for those in leadership (which could include just about everyone in one form or another—a mother is a leader to her children, etc.)—"**Without consultation, plans are frustrated, but with many counselors they succeed**" (Proverbs 15:22).

In his commentary on Proverbs, John Phillips says, "*It is foolhardy to act without knowing all the facts. It is sensible to get a second opinion. It is sensible to consider that opinion even when it differs materially from our own. It is sensible to evaluate other points of view and to weigh all the evidence. Then, even if we do make a wrong decision, we will make an honest mistake.*"[1] Phillips makes some valid points. And while leaders are, on occasion, called to make snap decisions and do not always have the luxury of examining all the facts, most issues we face can wait for further scrutiny.

When we do have the time to analyze our decisions it is wise to get the opinions and advice of other godly men and women. And let me stop right here and make a strong suggestion to the men who are reading this: Don't make the mistake of only getting input from the other men around you. Women are wired differently than men by the plan and purpose of God. They have the ability to look at a situation from a totally different angle and perspective than men do. Not soliciting their advice or totally

---

[1] John Phillips, *Exploring Proverbs, Volume 1,* (Grand Rapids: Kregel Academic & Professional, 2002).

ignoring what they have to say without weighing it properly is a massive mistake. Get input from as many godly sources as you possibly can when time allows, and include godly women.

The problem is that, most of us, especially men, try to go it alone when it comes the time to make decisions. There is an old saying that agrees with our Proverb—*"Self-advised is ill-advised."* Making plans without input from others is foolish. That input can come from many sources. We have the benefit of good books, CDs, DVDs, podcasts, etc., all of which can be used in the context of **many counselors**. Don't ignore the godly people you can talk to face-to-face but realize that good advice can come from a book or other media sources.

Finally, do not forget or ignore the ultimate source of wisdom and knowledge—God. God is available to each of us at any time of the day or night. He is there to give us advice through the Scriptures, through prayer, and through His Holy Spirit. This should always be the very first place you go. When you have a major decision to make, bring it before the Lord in prayer and then search the Scriptures. If you genuinely seek God's advice and give Him proper time to answer, even if things seem to be going wrong from a human perspective, the decision will have been the right one.

Don't do it alone when decisions need to be made.

Ultimately, which will be harder—accepting advice and/or constructive criticism or ignoring it? Humble yourself or be humbled is the moral of this story.

Let me share a Christmas memory of mine. My wife's sister and family were in town, visiting over one Christmas holiday. It was Christmas Eve and both of our young boys were fast asleep, which means time for the dads to assemble all the toys that were going to be under the tree. My brother-in-law and I had a wonderful time of fellowship as we dove into the task at hand. I don't remember the items we were assembling but I do remember, after several attempts at doing it alone, we finally broke out the instructions and got things put together in the wee hours of the morning.

It was fun, but it could have been done quicker if we had followed the instructions from the onset.

I don't know if Solomon struggled with this aspect of manhood early on, but, according to our Proverb, he did figure things out eventually—"**Those who listen to instruction will prosper; those who trust the Lord will be happy**" (Proverbs 16:20, author's paraphrase).

Why is it that people in general and men in particular resist following instructions? There are exceptions, but most try to do things their own way before finally getting the help that is readily available to them. Would it change our attitudes and actions to know that God promises success to those who follow instruction? Before you answer that, let's make sure we have the proper context of this.

First, the overall context of the Book of Proverbs is that of gaining wisdom. More specifically, we are to pursue godly wisdom at all costs. Next, when we look at the literal translation from the Hebrew of this first phrase, it says, "*Being wise about the word he will find good.*" When you tie these two together, you will begin to get a clearer picture of what is being taught. The promise of success comes from following God's Word or His instructions. We must also be careful concerning the word translated as **"prosper"**—God is not promising wealth to those who follow His word; He is promising success, or good, in general terms.

But, just in case we did not take the time to consider the context of this opening phrase by going back and by researching the original language, Solomon then adds, "**those who trust the Lord will be happy.**" So, while there is something to be said for following general instructions, God is not necessarily promising success in doing so; He is making that promise for those who follow the instructions of His Word.

I can't resist making an obvious observation. The only way we can follow God's instructions is to know what they are in the first place. And the only way we will know what they are is to read them. So, the success and happiness of our Christian lives is predicated on the amount of time we spend reading and doing what God says. And yes, it is really that simple—so get busy!

The value of wisdom

In Proverbs 16:16 (author's paraphrase), we get another admonition to pursue wisdom—"**How much better to get wisdom than gold, and understanding than silver!**"

Gaining wisdom and understanding is a multifaceted quest. Solomon uses gold and silver in his analogy, but he repeats himself often in this book. The illustration of a diamond may be helpful. I've never paid much attention to diamonds (that's my wife's job) but I do know that one of the attractions is the cut. The symmetry and design of the many cuts or surfaces on a well-crafted diamond plays a major role in its value. All of these cuts bring out the brilliance of the stone, and, at the proper angle, will reflect all the colors of the rainbow. Gaining true wisdom and understanding is similar; we must look at it from all angles to see all the beauty.

We know this truth. We know that God's wisdom, understanding, and discernment are priceless. We know that we should pursue gaining these qualities above all other pursuits in our lives. God's Word has proven itself to us time and time again. God's principles have come through in our lives without fail. The wisdom from the pages of Scripture has been, and always will be, timeless. We know this beyond any doubt. Yet we rarely act as if it is true.

Let me explain why I say this. When tough times come our way on a financial level, what do we do? We put our minds to the task of worrying, and then figuring out what we can do to get more money (gold and silver). Our thoughts are consumed with money. Our words are filled with money. Our actions are based upon money (or lack thereof). We analyze our situation, we cut corners where corners can be cut, we think of what can be sold, we consider taking on another job, and then we analyze the situation some more. All the while, God is gently calling, "**How much better to get wisdom than gold, and understanding than silver.**" But our minds are so consumed with our problem that there is no room to add, or even hear a word from God.

Beloved, we cannot miss the importance of this Proverb. If we can grasp all the implications it carries, and if we can view and admire all the facets as if we were examining a perfectly cut diamond, then we will be on the path to true wisdom and understanding. The trials and troubles of this life would no longer faze us because they are simply another perfectly crafted cut in the diamond. All of the traps and snares of Satan would be so very obvious and plain before us. We would essentially have "new eyes" that could see the world and see eternity from God's vantage point. And it is ours for the taking if we would just apply ourselves to its study.

Most Christians are facing a crisis. We are lacking or even bankrupt of wisdom and understanding. If we would only see this, and if we would only apply as much analyzing and concern and time over our lack of biblical wisdom as we do our lack of gold and silver, we would immediately see what has true and lasting value.

So, before skipping ahead to read the chapters that more specifically cover the Proverbs that are focused on finances, please understand that, apart from the foundations being laid in these opening chapters, your attempted applications of *only* the verses that speak directly to financial concerns will give you short-lived results at best.

* * *

TAKE ACTION

Commit to reading one chapter of Proverbs every day for the rest of your days to ensure that you are continuously obtaining God's wisdom.

CHAPTER 2

FIRST THINGS FIRST

S ince you made the decision to read this book, I know you are likely chomping at the bit to find the *"five easy steps"* to solving all of your money problems. First of all, you are not going to find five easy steps, or ten for that matter; following the advice from the Book of Proverbs on handling your finances is more substantive than that and requires real change from the current accepted practices. Secondly, you really need to either develop or review several character traits taught to us in this tremendous Book of the Bible or the financial advice will likely be of little or no value.

This chapter deals with foundational issues like character, integrity, and reputation; apart from which it will be extremely difficult to apply and maintain God's principles on money. So, if you desire to glean the most from this book, please bear with me and, again, resist the urge to skip ahead.

Character

At my first "serious" job (9–5, Monday–Friday kind of job), I worked in a division of a company where we created and tested prototypes of catalytic converters. We were a small group of guys—I think nine of us including the two bosses. One of the guys in the group had one of the filthiest minds and mouths I had ever encountered up until that time. As a young man who had not reached any real level of spiritual maturity yet, I did not always walk away or tell this guy that I didn't want to hear his dirty jokes and sexual innuendos—consequently, some of that filth is still etched into the recesses of my mind forty years later.

I don't remember his name, but I do remember that he was always in some sort of trouble—trouble at work, trouble at home, and trouble with his relationships in general. He was not a happy man. His only cause for laughter and the only times I saw him smile was while he was telling or listening to dirty jokes.

I didn't stay at that company for very long, so I don't know what became of him, but our next Proverb gives me a good idea; unless, at some point after I left the company, he turned away from his sin and turned to the Lord—**"He who has a crooked mind ... and he who is perverted in his language falls into evil"** (17:20).

The Bible tells us that **"The heart is more deceitful than all else and is desperately sick"** (Jeremiah 17:9). In context, Jeremiah is contrasting the person who places his trust in mankind with those who place their trust in God. When we place our trust in mankind and the things of this world, we are allowing our hearts to deceive us. The world tells us that indulging in its pleasures is not only a good thing to do but the right thing to do. But if we only depend on our own understanding (our own heart) as Proverbs 3:5–6 speaks about and ignore or refuse to consult God's wisdom (the principles in the Bible), we will be deceived.

I am constantly hearing well-intentioned Christians say things that are not biblical. The words that come out of their mouths sound good from a human perspective, and maybe even sound good from a Christian perspective, but the concepts they are placing their hope and trust in are either not in the Bible or are being taken out of context (which also means they are not in the Bible). At these times, we are allowing our hearts to deceive us, and a deceptive, crooked heart will not prosper. We will be disappointed when things turn south, and some will even begin to doubt their faith and turn away from God, but we set ourselves up for failure when we follow our hearts and follow worldly wisdom in spiritual matters.

Bad things happen in this world even to God-fearing, Bible-reading, committed Christians. Jobs are lost, cars break down, loved ones die, and relationships are broken. Claiming that you will always keep your job, or that your car will miraculously fix itself, or that your loved ones will be healed and live forever, or that your broken relationships will be mended is a claim from your (deceitful) heart and not a claim you can make from Scripture. Yes, God can step in and take care of all of these situations and much more, but it is not a promise that we can claim in this life. As a matter of fact, we can claim the exact opposite (2 Timothy 3:12). If you live a godly life, you will suffer for it, and this is God's will for you (1 Peter 3:17; 4:19; 5:10). But in the suffering, God will make you strong and mature in Christ Jesus (James 1:2–4).

Trust in the Lord and not in your heart. Make sure you can back up the words you speak with the words God has already spoken. In this way, you will prosper; in this way, you will avoid tumbling into trouble; in this way, you will develop character; and, in this way, you keep your faith strong. This important aspect of a person's life can and needs to be developed and cultivated and protected. Even if you were not necessarily raised in an environment that encouraged strong character, you can develop one.

Do the right thing

Doing the right thing, though, is not always easy. Unless you are a very mature Christian, doing the right thing is rarely easy. The temporary *benefits* of not doing the right thing will often outweigh the lasting *consequences* of doing the right thing. From a worldly mindset, it is often much easier to justify your wrong deeds than to make the hard decision to do the right thing. Our next Proverb reinforces the concept of choosing what is right—"**To do righteousness and justice is desired by the Lord more than sacrifice**" (21:3).

King Saul faced the choice of doing the right thing or almost doing the right thing. He was to attack and utterly destroy the Amalekites—men, women, children, cattle, sheep, etc. No life was to be spared because of the sins they had committed against God and against His people. Saul wiped out almost all of the people (he spared the king and, apparently, a few others) and he kept some of the choicest sheep and cattle. When the Lord's prophet, Samuel, confronted Saul, his excuse was he kept the animals to sacrifice to the Lord—he justified his disobedience.

Samuel's reply is found in 1 Samuel 15:22–23: **"Has the Lord as much delight in burnt offerings and sacrifices as in obeying the voice of the Lord? Behold, to obey is better than sacrifice, and to heed than the fat of rams. For rebellion is as the sin of divination, and insubordination is as iniquity and idolatry. Because you have rejected the word of the Lord, He has also rejected you from being king."**

Every time we cut corners, and every time we almost obey God, or partially obey God, we are as disobedient as King Saul. After this last incident with Saul's disobedience, God removed His blessing from the king, and the process began for the kingdom being removed from Saul and from the succeeding generations of his family—and, by the way, the Amalekites that escaped propagated and eventually birthed the evil Haman from the Book of Esther. Haman almost succeeded in having the Jews exterminated in the entire kingdom of his time.

All sin is an affront to our holy God, but the Scripture is clear that God has stronger hatred, if you will, to a handful of sins. Witchcraft and idolatry are two of the biggies, and God views rebellion and insubordination in the same light as witchcraft and idolatry. This should not only get our attention, but it should shake us to the core of our being. The rebel heart is nothing to take casually or lightly.

Under the Law of Moses, witchcraft and idolatry were capital offences, meaning that the penalty for such sins was death by stoning. Yet another reason for us to praise God for the gift of grace, but not even close to reason enough to casually brush aside our rebellion and insubordination or stubbornness. Witchcraft flies in the face of God as does rebellion.

Insubordination and stubbornness are as idolatry because we make ourselves to be a god when determining our way to be better than God's way.

One of the catchphrases I bought into and clung to as a rebel in my own right was, *"It's easier to ask forgiveness than permission."* And I thought that was perfectly okay to not only have that attitude but to operate under that premise.

I knew my Bible, but, like so many Christians, I was woefully inept at applying its principles to my life. My rebel heart was not always in open defiance of the Bible, but I was lacking in intentionally making choices and decisions fully based on Scripture. I was, at times, ignorant and, at other times, overtaken by my rebel heart, but I was never intentionally searching the Scriptures for the basis in operating my every decision.

God does not want our offerings and sacrifices if they are replacing obedience. We cannot cover up our sin by making sacrifices to God or putting money in the offering plate. God wants our obedience and He wants it 100% and without excuse or justification. He could care less about our sacrifices and offerings if they do not come from a pure, righteous, and sincere heart. The prophet Amos even goes so far as to say that God rejects our singing of praise and worship when it comes from a disobedient heart—**"Take away from Me the noise of your songs; I will not even listen to the sound of your harps"** (Amos 5:23).

God hates religion. Religion is man attempting to please God in his own way. God does not want that—He simply wants obedience to His ways. If you truly want to please the Lord, He tells us how in His Word. Solomon boils it all down with his last words in the Book of Ecclesiastes: **"The conclusion, when all has been heard, is: fear God and keep His commandments, because this applies to every person. For God will bring every act to judgment, everything which is hidden, whether it is good or evil"** (Ecclesiastes 12:13–14).

Fear God and obey His commands—this is far better than your gifts and sacrifices; and please do not expect financial blessing without obedience to God's Word already the major focus of your life. Financial gain can and does come to some who have no regard for God or the Scripture, but the true and eternal blessing is nonexistent and impossible to obtain.

Pursue integrity

When I was just a child, my father had to work two and sometimes three jobs to make ends meet. We weren't necessarily poor, but he struggled to keep our standard of living up to par. Because my dad had to work so much, it was not common for him to be able to attend my baseball games. But, when he did get to come, I remember waiting to hear from him that I did a good job even if I struck out three times. There is something within each of us that longs for the approval of our parents. When we don't get that approval, it is almost as if we are trapped in a personal prison cell of sorts—we cannot go free until we get that approval we long for. Even if I did strike out three times, if dad said I tried my best, I could go home with head held high.

Here's a sobering thought: Our heavenly Father never misses an event in our lives. He is right there watching over us; not only at special events, but He is there for absolutely everything you and I do; He doesn't miss anything. Our heavenly Father is there whether we are willfully in sin or we are living according to His Word. And He has an opinion of both—"**The perverse in heart are an abomination to the Lord, but the blameless in their walk are His delight**" (Proverbs 11:20).

When my dad attended my games, I tried extra hard to do my best. And, quite honestly, that was all that mattered—that my genuine effort was there. That is the same thing our heavenly Father is looking for—our genuine effort to follow His way for our lives. God isn't looking for us to hit homeruns all the time; the outward results are His anyway. It is the inward character and integrity that are **His delight**. This is not an excuse to fall short on obedience to God's Word, only that we will not always perfectly execute His commands. On the other hand, He is disgusted with those who are **perverse in heart**, or those who lack moral character and integrity.

So, what are the results of our choices—"**Assuredly, the evil man will not go unpunished, but the descendants of the righteous will be delivered**" (Proverbs 11:21).

When you live an evil life, a life with no regard to God, He will eventually exact His divine and righteous judgment. It doesn't always happen immediately—some will not reap the consequences of their actions until the final judgment—but they will pay for the error of their ways eventually. Those who live lives of obedience to His will—**the righteous, will be delivered**, or receive eternal reward from God.

Since our heavenly Father is watching over us at all times, let's continually do our best to please Him—just like that little boy who struck out all too often.

Integrity in speech

I remember a line in a movie I once saw. One of the characters in the movie asked, "*How did you know he was lying?*" The other character answered, "*Because his lips were moving.*"

Talk is cheap, as the expression goes, but following through with promised actions is becoming much rarer in our society. In the Middle Eastern culture, to which Solomon originally wrote this to, talk was very cheap. They had a series of phrases and actions they took to convey the level of truthfulness they were held to. If they didn't "swear" by a certain thing, they felt that they were not held to keep that promise. It is kind of like us today saying, "I swear to God" or "I swear on my mother's grave," etc. The bad thing about having to say something like that is the implication is that everything else you've said up until that point has been a lie. You imply that you cannot be trusted unless you say something like "I swear to God," but, effectively, you imply that you can rarely if ever be trusted.

Jesus addressed this very issue when speaking to the pharisees in Matthew 23:16–22. "**Woe to you, blind guides, who say, 'Whoever swears by the temple, that is nothing; but whoever swears by the gold in the** temple is obligated.' You fools and blind men! Which is more important, the gold or the temple that sanctified the gold? And, 'Whoever swears by the altar, that is nothing, but whoever swears by the offering on it, he is obligated.' You blind men, which is more important, the offering, or the altar that sanctifies the offering? Therefore, whoever swears by the altar, swears both by the altar and by everything on it. And whoever swears by the temple, swears both by the temple and by Him who dwells in it. And whoever swears by heaven, swears both by the throne of God and by Him who sits upon it."

Jesus was not giving a formula for skirting the truth but was simply making the point that truthfulness and integrity are not commodities to be loosely traded; you either have full integrity or you have none.

Proverbs 12:22 forever links our words with our actions—"**Lying lips are an abomination to the Lord, but those who deal faithfully are His delight.**" Notice how the initial subject is your words (**lying lips**) but the second half of the Proverb deals with your actions (**those who deal faithfully**). Our words and our actions should always go hand-in-hand. We should never have to make an excuse for why we did not follow through with what we said we would do.

The problem that exists is that most people (including Christians) do not look at their lack of following through as telling a lie. We seem to feel that, since our original intentions were good, when circumstances or personal preference gets in the way of following through, it's no big deal. But, in reality, we lied! It may not have been a lie when we originally committed ourselves to some action, but, when we failed to follow through, it became a lie. And "**lying lips are an abomination to the Lord.**" We must see our lack of following through for what it is—sin! We must be known as people who can be counted upon to keep our word. Other people should never have to even give it a second thought when we say we will do something for them—it should be as good as done in their minds.

Without complete integrity, you will not be in the position for God to fully bless your financial pursuits, at least not to the extent that God has in store. When we follow through and put actions behind our words, we not only will gain the respect of people, but we gain the **delight** of the Lord. And how great is it to know that the Lord delights in you? So, be sure to only say what you intend to follow through with, and quickly make amends when the inevitable emergency does preclude you from keeping your vow. Your words and your deeds need to be one and the same.

Be genuine

I have no idea how close the crime shows on television come to real life—so, this illustration may be less than I intend it to be, but, on TV, the various crime dramas examine a crime scene, analyze the evidence they have discovered, and pinpoint a suspect. But before they go to court, they look for a motive—why did this person commit this crime? Without a strong motive, sometimes the evidence they have is not enough for a conviction in the eyes of the jury. It is human nature for us to want to know why. Motive can sometimes make all the difference in the world in obtaining a conviction—at least on TV.

Proverbs 13:7, once you have gone beyond the surface, deals with the motive of a person's heart—"**There is one who pretends to be rich, but has nothing; another pretends to be poor, but has great wealth.**" The implication from Solomon is that both sides of this Proverb point out sin in a person's life. Whether you are poor or rich, it is a sin to pretend to be the opposite. Underneath this deception, you will inevitably find improper motives.

The great puritan commentator, Matthew Henry, dissects this verse with a two-pronged approach—a man's physical position in life (or worldly estate as Henry puts it) and a man's spiritual position in life. I wish to follow this same approach.

If we look at this Proverb purely from the viewpoint of a man's worldly estate, what sinful motives could we uncover for pretending to be someone you are not?

A materially poor man who pretends to be rich will either be under the control of the sin of pride or the sin of coveting. Pride shows up by simply wanting other people to think you are someone of note. You are living above your means solely for the purpose of how the world views you. You may drive a Lexus when all you can really afford is a Chevy. You may have a 4,000-square-foot house when you should be in a 1,500-square-foot house—you are driven by pride to keep up your appearances. Coveting appears when the one who puts on this show looks for an opportunity to swindle or steal from those who are truly rich. This person wants what the others have.

A materially rich man who pretends to be poor is primarily under the control of the sin of greed. This person is afraid of losing what he has—either from someone stealing it or from those who would come to him for a donation. If he can just put on the front of not having much, people will leave him alone. He can keep all that he has for himself.

Most of us are neither rich nor poor, so the application from a worldly perspective is to be genuine in whom we are. Looking at our Proverb from a spiritual perspective is something we can all gain from.

A spiritually poor man (one who is not saved) who pretends to be rich (a true Christian) is primarily wishing to portray a moral and righteous character to be accepted by the church he attends. He wants the prestige of being looked up to without having to change his life. He is a false Christian, which is no Christian at all. He seeks the applause of men. Some have even more nefarious motives and can be categorized as the "tares" that Jesus speaks of—unsaved people in the church putting on the act in order to look for opportunities to cause division.

A spiritually rich man who pretends to be poor is a coward. A true Christian has the riches of an inheritance with Christ. We are children of the King, heirs to the throne, joint-heirs with the Son, and we live like paupers. We live as if the temporary struggles of this life are a burden beyond our ability to bear. And, worse yet, by pretending to be spiritually poor, we are not exhibiting to the lost and dying world around us that we have the riches of Christ to share with them—we refuse to tell others about the free gift of God's salvation that we have and is available to them also. We greedily hang on to the riches we have, pretending to be poor.

Whatever state we find ourselves in, rich or poor materially or spiritually, we must be genuine about our identity. It is sin to act any other way and not only shows a complete lack of integrity, but also a lack of trust in God; and again, as we will discover later in the book, trust in God is a cornerstone in properly handling finances.

The incredible value of a good name

Integrity also marks your heritage, your reputation, your reliability, your name.

When you think about receiving an inheritance, I will assume that most, if not all, think in terms of monetary or material goods. And while Solomon may indeed be speaking in these terms, I believe his intent is much broader than just the material (the original Hebrew is not as clear as we would like it to be). We may not belong to a family that has been blessed with an abundance of money, yet they still could be people of great moral character in the sense I believe Solomon intends.

Solomon says, "**A good man leaves an inheritance to his children's children, and the wealth of the sinner is stored up for the righteous**" (Proverbs 13:22). I think the Amplified Bible captures the essence of this verse—"**A good man leaves an inheritance [of moral stability and goodness] to his children's children, and the wealth of the sinner [find its way eventually] into the hands of the righteous, for whom it was laid up.**" In this translation, we see that the inheritance Solomon is probably speaking of is the inheritance of a good name—of a heritage of righteousness and integrity.

How important is a good name or legacy of righteousness in a family? I come from a family that never had much in the way of money. There are a few on my mom's side who have enough to live comfortably and will probably be able to pass some material wealth on to their children, but, by and large, both sides of my family will be fortunate if they have enough to live on when retirement comes. But there are several pastors, deacons, and upstanding moral Christian people generously sprinkled on both sides of my family. There is a heritage of living according to the principles of God that has been passed down through the years. This **inheritance** of godliness has been passed down to me.

A good name and a godly heritage are a treasure that is worth more than gold and silver. A good Christian friend and I were talking on the phone a while back. His ninety-year-old grandmother was in the hospital for the last time. She was a Christian and seemed more than ready to see her Lord and be reunited with her mother in heaven. As our conversation continued, my friend began to speak about how many of her children and grandchildren are following God, and how they are hungry to know more about Jesus. Now that's an inheritance that lasts!

Some of you may not have come from a long line of Christian people in your family. Some are maybe even embarrassed to talk about your family history. If that's the case with you, then let the godly heritage in your family begin with you. Let your children and your grandchildren become the beneficiaries of a godly inheritance. Even people with good Christian family ties have some bad eggs. My father did a search of his family tree a while back and he was pretty sure that one of our ancestors was hanged for stealing a horse. Your family background does not define who you are—you can start fresh and see God's blessings filter down through the ensuing generations.

So, be thankful for your inheritance from God, and work on leaving behind a godly heritage for your family and the future generations that will follow. You will be developing the character and qualities that are necessary to honor God in your financial life.

Yet another Proverb reinforces this concept of how vital a good name is—"**A good name is to be more desired than great wealth, favor is better than silver or gold**" (Proverbs 22:1).

The old saying, *"You can't judge a book by its cover"* is typically very true, but the public does indeed judge a book by its cover. Notice the next time you walk through a bookstore. The bestselling authors have their names in big, bold letters on the cover of the book, and often, their picture, while lesser known or unknown author's names are in much smaller print with the title or the cover art being more prominent. But even with all of these marketing tricks, you still cannot tell how good the book is by its cover alone. Well-known authors can write a bad novel and unknown authors can write a fantastic one, but you have to go beyond the surface to find out.

On the surface, having great wealth may seem to be something of greater value than a good reputation, but God's Word disagrees.

Many of you are contemplating in your mind right now the veracity of this Proverb. You are weighing the two choices as if they are indeed choices for you right now: *"Would I rather have unbelievable riches or a good reputation?"* If you did have the choice, Solomon (and God) says having a good reputation and being held in high esteem is far better than having great wealth. Why?

You have to dig below the surface, or go beyond just looking at the cover, to truly understand the value of a thing as opposed to just the cost of a thing. Now, obviously, it is possible to have a good reputation AND great wealth, but, if a choice has to be made, what is the value of each individually, and why does Solomon choose the one over the other?

Solomon knew from experience both conditions. He was the wealthiest man to ever walk this planet and he was the wisest and most highly esteemed person of the world as well. But Solomon allowed his reputation to be tarnished in a big way. He began to live his life in any way he pleased, and he indulged in every carnal obsession known to man. Pleasure became his god and no longer did the kings and queens of earth come to him for advice.

Riches and material wealth come, and they go just as quickly; these are not something that last. You can have wealth one moment, lose it the next, and regain it again. A good reputation can be destroyed in one fleeting moment and never be regained. Just ask the many prominent pastors and evangelists who have fallen into public sin and ridicule. Some of them have gone on to start new ministries or pastor a church once again, but their reputations will always have a cloud over them.

Protect your reputation as much as you would protect a room full of gold. On second thought, protect it more than you would a room full of gold.

Integrity in trying circumstances

There is a great moral dilemma that permeates the theme of most Hollywood movies—more so in the great movies of bygone eras, but still to a lesser degree even today. If you watch closely, there will always be a choice that one or more of the main characters must make. The choice will usually involve something that benefits their own happiness, financial well-being, or social status, but, in making that choice, they have to do something dishonest or illegal. If they choose to do the right thing, they risk losing the worldly benefit that presents itself before them. In the "old days," the characters would almost invariably choose to do the right thing after some internal deliberations. In today's movies, you just never know.

Solomon places this dilemma in our laps today by leaving no doubt as to which choice we should always make—"**Better is little with righteousness than great income with injustice**" (Proverbs 16:8).

Unlike the movies, the scales in real life seem to be tilted in favor of doing the illegal and/or the dishonest in order to gain personal benefit—unfortunately, even amongst many who claim to be Christians, especially when it comes to issues where the person feels that nobody is looking, or their decision doesn't directly affect the lives or well-being of another individual. The obvious example is when you prepare your taxes each year. Since such a small percentage of tax returns get audited each year, fudging a few numbers to enhance your tax bill or tax refund doesn't seem to be such a bad thing. Nobody is watching and you aren't directly hurting any one person in particular when you cheat.

Obviously, you are hurting yourself when you choose the dishonest route in anything, and others, eventually, are hurt as well. In our tax example, you are now living with an unconfessed sin in your life, and—regardless of your feelings about government corruption and whether or not they deserve your tax dollars—when tax revenues are down because of fraudulent returns, social programs get cut and other people are indeed affected by your sin.

In God's eyes, it is much better to do the right thing regardless of the personal consequences. And don't just think of taxes in this moral dilemma. Think of what's right when faced with telling the truth or telling a lie. Think of what's right when you are responsible for accidentally damaging someone else's property when no one is looking. Think of what is right when you stumble upon some information that wasn't meant for you at the office or workplace, etc.

It doesn't matter how large the personal benefit may be, in the long run, it will not be worth it. And we have another Proverb that essentially teaches this same principle: **"Better is a poor man who walks in his integrity than he who is perverse in speech and is a fool"** (Proverbs 19:1).

Scandals in business, in government, and in churches prove that integrity is a concept that is much easier talked about and promoted than actually put into practice. Ask any business owner, politician, or church leader if they believe in integrity and you will undoubtedly get a positive and emphatic "Yes!" But, as we have already mentioned, "Talk is cheap."

Solomon states that honest poverty is better than dishonest wealth. And by this, he says that wealth and possessions are not the measure of life's worth and value. Truth, justice, and righteousness are far more important in this life than the things you can touch, taste, see, smell, and hear. Integrity is of infinitely more value than a large bank account or a house full of possessions.

We live in a "material world" as pop singer, Madonna, sang in the '80s, but, when this life is over, all things material will be of no value—zero! As one preacher said, *"I've never seen a hearse pulling a U-Haul."* So, if material things are of no eternal value, why do most of us spend our lives desiring them and accumulating them?

Material possessions and/or wealth are not inherently wrong, but we must be very careful in our own self-evaluations. If you lined up every

Christian on the planet and asked to step forward those who think they have abused the privilege God has given them in accumulating material things, I would be surprised if very many actually stepped forward. We could all point out people who should step forward, but it certainly isn't me!

Yet God speaks of money and possessions more than any other topic in the Bible. I fear that most Christians, especially in our culture, have been deceived when it comes to their possessions and money. They have blurred the line between wants and needs. They have fallen for the world's assertion that you deserve everything you can get. We have sold out. Our integrity is most likely lacking when it comes to the stewardship of God's provision.

If God impressed upon you to give $100 to someone in need the next time you were out, could you do it? Now, $100 means more to some than others, so it is probably not a fair test, but choose the amount that would typically be a stretch for you. I only use this example because it happened to me many years ago—and I failed miserably! I resisted God's impression upon my heart to give away the hundred-dollar bill I had in my pocket. My Christian integrity was weighed in the scales found wanting as I ignored the Spirit's leading and held on to my hundred-dollar bill. I have since learned from that lesson, but I struggle with the material trap along with the rest of you.

We are so blessed in this country and yet we are so out of line in our accumulation of things. Our Christian integrity is compromised almost every time we accumulate unnecessary "stuff."

Integrity—we all could stand to dwell on that word a little more. Then we could all stand to see where it needs to be applied to our lives—and it needs to be applied in every area of our lives, not just in our handling of money and possessions.

So, what's your price to damage or destroy your integrity? Many years ago, I asked this question as part of a sermon (What's your price?). If I remember correctly, the context for the question involved our Christian testimony and taking a stand for Jesus Christ regardless of the situation.

I believe I asked the question something like this: *"What's your price to deny Jesus before others?"* One person caught me after the service to say no price could get them to deny Jesus. A week or two later, this same person pulled me aside almost in tears to tell me, *"I discovered my price this week, and it was ugly."*

This next Proverb asks the same question—**"To show partiality is not good, because for a piece of bread a man will transgress"** (Proverbs 28:21).

Even though the actual question is not stated, the implication of this Proverb is one of having a price for doing something of questionable character, or, more simply, of taking a bribe. The fact of the matter is that the bribe is of very little value, meaning mankind tends to sell his dignity and character for pennies—in this instance, **a piece of bread**.

Judas Iscariot sold out the King of kings and Lord of lords for thirty pieces of silver; the price to buy a common slave in that time. Many Christians sell their testimony and witness for the price of being part of the crowd. Some sell their integrity for a few bucks on their tax return. Others sell their purity for a few moments of pleasure. Almost invariably, we sell something of tremendous value at garage sale prices. I want to say we sell our character and our integrity and our purity and our testimony on the clearance rack of life, but that example is too clean and antiseptic for what it truthfully is—it is more like selling something in a back alley where no one can witness it and where value is discounted even more.

So, what is your character worth? What is your integrity worth? What is your purity worth? What is your witness and testimony worth? Will a piece of bread do the trick? Or maybe you require a whole meal.

I know these are tough and weighty words, but this is what Solomon is trying to get through to us. We must be careful to make sure we place the proper value on our lives and the things that truly matter. You (and that means everything about you and everything you are) are of infinite value in the eyes of God. He sacrificed His most valuable possession for you. He sent His only Son to this earth to live a sinless life and then suffer a horrendous day of torture and death—for you! To purchase you! To be able to call you His son or daughter! From a human perspective, it makes you think God made a horrible deal, but, from God's perspective, He paid the exact price and received great value in return. You are of immeasurable worth!

This is how valuable you are in the eyes of God, and this is the kind of value you must place on your integrity and your purity and your character and your witness and testimony and everything else that you are. Don't sell yourself short. Don't sell the priceless diamond that you are for a piece of bread—and maybe that's a good image to help you in this struggle. Picture your character as a truckload of priceless jewels, your integrity as a room full of silver, your purity as vault full of diamonds, and your witness and testimony as all of Solomon's gold.

Would you sell any of those for a piece of bread?

We have laid down a few foundation stones that are required to truly build upon, to be prepared for God's principles in handling wealth. If you attempt to apply anything else in this book by shortcutting or ignoring the character in you that God requires, you will be disappointed. Don't be in too much of a rush to straighten out everything in your financial life; you obviously did not get in a mess overnight and there are likely many causes. If needed, reread this chapter, jot down some notes, and make any necessary changes here before moving on. With the proper foundation, you can build a new and lasting financial existence.

* * *

TAKE ACTION

Develop the resolve to be a man or woman of complete integrity. Ask for the Holy Spirit's help, then make it a habit to pause before every decision and action to give time for you to evaluate what you are about to do. Work on yourself and your character as much or more than you work on your goals and pursuits.

CHAPTER 3

THE FOUR-LETTER
WORD TO EMBRACE

Mention work to the people you come in contact with today and you will likely get all manner of negative comments. Even those who enjoy their jobs will typically join in on the jokes and disparaging comments about work.

In the midst of a somewhat recent economic downturn, a good friend set the record straight when a mutual friend interrupted a conversation we were all enjoying by saying, "*Well, I hate to cut this short, but I **have** to go to work.*" My friend jumped in with a big smile on his face and corrected our mutual friend by saying, "*No, you **get** to go to work!*"

The Bible has much to say on the topic of work and it's all from a positive viewpoint with the notable exception that the fall in the Garden of Eden has made it more difficult to accomplish. From the beginning, work was created by and ordained by God. Work is good and a good worker should be one of the identifying marks of a Christian.

On being a good employee

"Like vinegar to the teeth and smoke to the eyes, so is the lazy one to those who send him" (Proverbs 10:26).

This Proverb is very vivid for me (and no, not because I'm lazy—well, not always). I cannot handle cigarette smoke. It gives me a headache, it makes my sinuses clog up, and it makes my eyes burn. Also, I have three teeth that are very sensitive; when I drink something cold or hot, or chew on something sweet, and let it get into that area of my mouth—YIKES! I've never described it as setting my teeth on edge, but that is a decent description.

Solomon is attempting to give each of us the wisdom to be a good employee (or servant) by showing us how our employer or leader can feel about us when we don't give an honest day's work or don't put forth a good effort in our volunteer labors.

Have you ever considered yourself as smoke in someone's eyes or vinegar on their teeth? I have never considered myself in such terms, but I must admit that there have been times when I did not give a full day's work on the job. Sometimes, I did not feel well; other times, I was angry at the boss; and still other times, I was simply lazy. None of these excuses cut it with God. We obviously are not going to be at our best when sick, but, if we are well enough to show up to get our hours recorded, we are well enough to put in a good effort.

Colossians 3:23 tells us that, when we are working for someone, we are to work as if the Lord was our boss—**"Whatever you do, do your work heartily, as for the Lord rather than for men."**

The passage in Colossians continues—**"knowing that from the Lord you will receive the reward of the inheritance. It is the Lord Christ whom you serve. For he who does wrong will receive the consequences of the wrong which he has done, and that without partiality"** (Colossians 3:24–25).

Whoever your boss or leader is in human terms, he or she are essentially a lower level immediate supervisor at best. God's Word says, **"It**

is the Lord Christ whom you serve"—you are working as for the Lord whether punching a time clock; receiving a salary; earning a commission; or volunteering your time to a church, ministry, or other organization. It doesn't matter what position you are in or even if you don't have an immediate boss or supervisor; if you are receiving compensation or you have volunteered your time, you qualify.

Knowing that Jesus is your boss, should that have an impact on your performance and your reliability? If you had to account for your time and effort to the Lord, would it change your approach, and would it increase your initiative to do an excellent job?

Regardless of the compensation allotted to you in this life, Jesus is keeping a divine ledger. The corners you cut and the wrong you do now will be recompensed in full by Him later. The effort you put forth to do and be your best now will be compensated in full later.

And we must notice that we do not have an exception in these verses. It doesn't tell us to work hard and be reliable only if our bosses are reasonable. 1 Peter 2:18–19 says, **"be submissive to your masters with all respect, not only to those who are good and gentle, but also to those who are unreasonable. For this finds favor, if for the sake of conscience toward God a person bears up under sorrows when suffering unjustly."** So, even if our bosses are unreasonable and ignorant, we do not have the right to work poorly or be lazy on the job—we must always keep in mind that our true boss and authority is God.

Evaluate your work ethic this week, whether you work an outside job, or you volunteer at your church—and make sure you are not smoke in your employer's eyes or vinegar on his or her teeth. Instead, be a diligent worker like an ant.

Have you ever played with ants? Try to block the progress of an ant and it will go around, go over, or go under. No obstacle will stop that ant from accomplishing its task; you will not stop an ant from reaching its goal apart from stepping on it.

If you have never played with or observed ants, how about this one: Have you ever been lazy? Have you ever given less than your best effort on the job because you just didn't feel like working that day? Have you ever neglected your responsibility in some area of life because you wanted to watch television? Have you ever …?

God, through his servant Solomon, gives us some wisdom concerning the effects of persistent laziness by teaching us a lesson from ants. Ants take full advantage of their situation. They don't waste time. The first warm day of spring, you will see ants going about their business.

Proverbs 6:6–11 says, "**Go to the ant, O sluggard, observe her ways and be wise, which having no chief, officer or ruler, prepares her food in the summer and gathers her provision in the harvest. How long will you lie down, O sluggard? When will you arise from your sleep? A little sleep, a little slumber, a little folding of the hands to rest – your poverty will come in like a vagabond and your need like an armed man.**"

Ants accomplish the task at hand and, if a crisis comes upon them, they immediately get to work—they don't get paralyzed with fear or anxiety and wonder what to do next. I used to cut grass for a living. Once in a while, I would come across a huge anthill in the middle of the lawn with my mower and the blades would chop the top off. One time, I stopped and watched them after taking the roof of their home off. They would all grab the food and the eggs and take them farther underground. No one was in a panic and no one was sitting back watching the others work. They had a task at hand, and it didn't matter how tired they were or what they were doing beforehand. They dropped everything and got to work.

Ants take advantage of the time they have. Ants are always of the mindset that winter is coming. And, since winter is indeed coming, they have to be about their business in the summer while they can. They instinctively know that the good times will not last—hard times are dead ahead, so they prepare.

In contrast, we have the sluggard or the lazybones. Instead of having the mindset of the ant (winter is coming), the mindset of the sluggard is that summer will last and last—*"I have plenty of time to prepare for winter, why work on such a beautiful day?"*

In John 9:4, Jesus said, "**We must work the works of Him who sent**

Me as long as it is day; night is coming when no one can work." The context in this verse obviously pertains to the work and ministry God gives for the Kingdom, but the application to our employment or business is also clear.

Obviously, there is a time to relax and have a lazy day, but too many of us have made it an art form. Take advantage of the time you have in the season in which you have it. *"You can't grow and harvest crops in the winter"* is the point Solomon makes for us. Take advantage of the opportunity you have while the opportunity exists.

Another example of taking advantage of opportunity when it avails itself is found from the excellent wife in Proverbs 31:24–25—**"She makes linen garments and sells them, and supplies belts to the tradesmen. Strength and dignity are her clothing, and she smiles at the future."**

Get your diploma, find a good company to work for, work your way through the ranks, retire with a nice pension, and ride off into the sunset, traveling the country in your RV. That was a reasonable plan fifty years ago, but it is a fairy tale today. The turnover even in established companies is ridiculous and pensions are all but extinct. The cycle has come around to finding your own way again as it was for all before the industrial age.

The Proverbs 31 woman would have had no problem with the times we live in—**"She makes them linen garments and sells them, and supplies belts to the tradesmen."** She was an entrepreneur before the term was created. She did not just make clothing for her family, but she made additional clothing to sell and create additional streams of income. She did not depend on some company or business owner to provide for her, she did not expect her government to give her a handout, and she did not even expect her husband to do all the providing; she used her God-given intellect, talents, and initiative to sell.

Sales has always been the most consistent means for income, often a very good income, yet it has somehow become a profession that most consider beneath them; most allow their pride to "protect" them from the damage to their fragile psyche when someone rejects their product or service. This is sad as the cycle of our economy and even the world economy is quickly swinging to sales and entrepreneurship as the primary means to earn an income.

The Proverbs 31 woman had no such hang-ups about sales, and, because of this attitude, **she smiles at the future**.

If you were to ask the women of this country what their view of the future was, I am sure it would be as varied as their hairstyles (and that was not a backhanded attempt at poking fun at all the hairstyles you ladies enjoy). I am sure some are very concerned about the future and I am sure many are confident and excited. I am also sure many are somewhere in between; maybe apprehensive would be a good descriptor.

But how many are smiling at the future? How many are so excited about what lies ahead that they can't wait to start the next day?

One of the core qualities of the Proverbs 31 woman is she is prepared for anything. The illustration of her clothing being **strength and dignity** shows us that she is fit for the task of taking on the challenges of the day. Her character denotes effective and enduring energy while, at the same time, showing how much she is set apart from the crowd. She is prepared, she is not afraid of selling or any other legitimate means of earning income, and God is her source of confidence.

Having this measure of preparation will undeniably lead you to having a confident attitude. Who would not be confident with an intimate knowledge of God as their source of confidence? So, regardless of the circumstances and situations all around your personal life and in this volatile and uncertain world, you can smile at the future.

If you allow your immediate circumstances to determine your joy and your attitude, you will be miserable often, and you will not have the capacity to smile at the future. If your immediate circumstances are controlling your joy and attitude, you are not trusting in God but trusting in your own ability to deal with the trials and struggles before you and that would be depressing!

So, build your foundation by building your relationship with the Lord; stop allowing others and your pride to dictate what is and is not the best way to earn an income; take advantage of opportunity, then crack a wide smile at the future!

On being a good boss

When you live in the mountains, as my wife and I do, you are exposed to a wide variety of God's wildlife. Over the time God has allowed us to live here, I have seen the following animals walking across my property: deer, elk, porcupine, bear, bobcat, lynx, mountain lion, llama, coyote, and a wide variety of more common varmints like squirrel, rabbit, chipmunk, field mouse, gopher, etc. While driving through our mountain community, I have also seen bighorn sheep, antelope, bison, cattle, and horses. Of all these species, the mountain lion is the most dangerous, followed by the bear. The mountain lions is the most dangerous because it will stalk and attack unprovoked at times if it deems you as small enough for it to take down. The bear is the most powerful but will not attack unless cornered, provoked, or feels her cubs are being threatened. I have accidentally come face-to-face with a bear (within ten feet) on two different occasions without any issue other than being scared out of my wits.

I have also learned that all of these animals can outrun me with the possible exception of the porcupine. I am sure, if I was ever in a situation where one of these more dangerous animals were pursuing me, I would still try to run—I'd just lose.

Solomon teaches us about an even more dangerous predator in today's Proverb—**"Like a roaring lion and a rushing bear is a wicked ruler over a poor people"** (Proverbs 28:15).

Any of us who has any level of authority over someone else falls under the category of a ruler in the context of this Proverb. The question then becomes, are you a kind and generous ruler or a wicked ruler? When you take advantage of your authority in any way you will be aligning yourself with the wicked. When you use your authority to accomplish what needs to be accomplished while, at the same time, helping and building up and promoting those who are deserving of such under your rule, you are ruling as God would have you to rule.

A parent who deals with his or her children in an abusive or threatening manner is a wicked ruler. A pastor who berates his flock is a wicked ruler. A supervisor or manager or boss of any kind who indiscriminately orders his or her employees around just to exert their power is a wicked ruler. A politician who uses his or her position for personal gain or to increase their power and standing is a wicked ruler.

The point is that, we should never use our positions of authority to cause harm to those under our authority—because with authority comes the power and the opportunity to uplift or destroy. A roaring lion and rushing bear have only one thing on their minds—to destroy.

John 10:10 says, "**The thief** (Satan) **comes only to steal and kill and destroy; I** (Jesus) **came that they may have life, and have it abundantly.**" So, to explain our Proverb in another way, when you take advantage of your position of authority at the expense of others, you are acting like Satan; when you rule righteously with the other's best interest at heart, you are acting like Jesus.

Do those under your authority come to you or do they run from you? And you do not need to be a corporate big shot to abuse even a self-appointed authority.

"A poor man who oppresses the lowly is like a driving rain which leaves no food" (Proverbs 28:3).

I recall hearing a story many years ago that went something like this:

Mr. Jones ran a tight ship as the office manager. A sixty-minute lunch break meant a sixty-minute lunch break, and everyone adhered to being back on time. One day, time got away from Mr. Jones while on his lunch hour and he arrived back to the office ten minutes late. No one said a word, but Mr. Jones was in a sour mood for the rest of the afternoon. In a twisted way of compensating for his tardiness, he was belligerent with his secretary who, in turn, quickly developed a sour attitude; the entire afternoon was miserable.

Quitting time came around and Mr. Jones's secretary fumed all the way home until she was at a fever pitch. When she arrived at her house, she immediately jumped all over her son who had left a mess in the kitchen and had not completed his daily chores. The son was now in a sour mood and stomped all over the house as he reluctantly took care of his daily duties. Frustrated and angry, the boy's cat made the mistake of walking in his path and the boy hauled off and kicked his cat.

Now, wouldn't it have been easier if Mr. Jones would have gone from his lunch break over to his secretary's house and kicked the cat himself?

No matter where we are stationed in life, we can always find someone or something that we can *be the boss of.* And the tendency is to take advantage of that position when we need to vent our anger.

What is it that causes us to vent our anger and frustration on people who have nothing to do with why we are feeling the way we do? You may have taken on more responsibility than you have time for, which leads to you being tired and tense, which leads to tossing and turning at night, which leads to being worn out, which leads to a bad attitude, which leads to saying or doing offensive things to innocent people, which leads to cats getting kicked—all because of something you started by making a foolish decision.

The illustration in our Proverb is one of something that should be a help turning into a disaster. Rain should cause the crops to grow and is obviously needed for the crops to grow. But if rain comes too fast and furious it can wash the crops away instead. In the same way, the people you are in contact with on a daily and weekly basis are very much needed for you to handle what this world throws at you. We are interdependent upon each other. We need human contact with friends, family, and even coworkers to help us deal with life. But, all too often, it only takes a moment in time to turn from being a very present help in a time of need to becoming an irritant that adds to the problem.

You have a greater effect on those around you than you probably realize. Your moods rub off on those around you. The expression, *"When momma ain't happy, ain't nobody happy"* is valid and true. People are naturally attracted to positive and happy people, and they are repelled by negative and grouchy people. Your attitude will affect the attitudes of those around you, and God is saying it is a disaster when you drag others down with you. You become the driving rain that washes all the crops away instead of the warm gentle rain that gives life to the crops.

The weight of financial concerns impacts your attitude and mood immensely. This burden will spill over into every relationship and responsibility if you do not purposely keep it separated from the other aspects of your daily life. You are taking the steps to gain control of your finances the way God directs by reading this book and investigating further the verses and passages that teach us. This won't happen quickly, but you will make progress and you should be able to relax a bit simply with this knowledge. So, keep your mood in check—the cats of the world, along with all of those around, will thank you.

On being fair in your dealings

I have a friend who frequently travels into foreign countries, and he has a lot of interesting stories. He tells me that, in many places outside the United States, everything that you would like to purchase has negotiable prices. In the States, we are accustomed to this concept when purchasing a car or a house, but, when we go to the store to buy a gallon of milk, or the department store to buy a pair of pants, we expect to pay what the price tag says. In many other corners of the world, the price listed is only a starting point for the negotiation.

The world has primarily operated on this principle from the beginning of time. Our American culture and way of doing things is only of recent times, relatively speaking. Just because we have set pricing in most of our purchases does not mean it is the only way or even the best way—it's simply our learned way.

Solomon speaks to this aspect of haggling and negotiating in this next Proverb—"**'Bad, bad,' says the buyer, but when he goes his way, then he boasts**" (Proverbs 20:14).

We can view the lesson Solomon is attempting to relate to us in two ways. First, he might be admonishing the buyers to be honest in their dealings. Don't berate the quality or the worth of a product for the sole purpose of getting a better deal. The second lesson could be for the sellers. Since no one in his right mind would brag about a terrible purchase, insight is needed when selling to a buyer who claims your product is worthless. Weigh their words carefully and understand the purpose of their tactics before settling on a price.

So, if you don't sell cars or houses for a living, how do you apply lessons like these, especially for those of us who live in the United States and rarely haggle over the price of an item?

The things you purchase are not the only things that you negotiate for in your life. You negotiate with your children (*"If you finish your chores, I'll go fishing with you."*). You negotiate with your boss (*"If you let me leave early today, I'll come in earlier tomorrow."*). You negotiate with your spouse (*"If you'll let me watch the game in peace, I'll clean out the garage when it's over."*). You negotiate with yourself (*"If you will exercise this morning, you can have that piece of cake this evening."*). And sadly, you negotiate with God (*"If You will get me out of this mess, I promise I'll go to church more, read my Bible more, etc."*).

Negotiations are a part of our everyday lives, even if we do not negotiate the price we pay for a loaf of bread. I believe the principle Solomon is trying to get across to us is to simply be honest in our negotiations. Don't take advantage of someone who is in a tight spot, regardless of whether you are the "buyer" or the "seller." And, if you do step over that line in good conscience, don't brag about your conquest.

But you might ask the following question—*"Technically speaking, if someone 'sells' to you at the price you want, how could that be considered taking advantage of them?"* After all, they could have said, *"No."* My response is simply this: Much more often than not, you know when you cross that line. You know when you have someone over a barrel. Giving someone a fair deal when you could rake them over the coals is the essence of this Proverb—and, remember, there are many applications and circumstances that you negotiate.

After all, we received more than a fair deal when Jesus paid for our sins—and that's the understatement of all time.

Being a fair negotiator is not the only way we avoid taking advantage of others.

Every now and then, America's southeast experiences a devastating hurricane season. When Katrina hit the gulf coasts of Louisiana, Alabama, and Mississippi, the destruction to homes, businesses, and lives was unprecedented in recent memory. The storm also took out or damaged many oil refineries in the area. As with most any natural disaster, we saw tremendous examples of mankind at their best. We also, unfortunately, saw some examples of mankind at their worst.

Many organizations and individuals, at their own personal expense, came to the aid of those who had lost everything. America opened their wallets and purses and donated as best they could to help those in need. Relief organizations assembled and mobilized to try and get to the hardest hit areas. People volunteered by the thousands to distribute food, water, medicine, clothing, and to help set up temporary housing. Churches organized groups of people and sent them down to help in any way they could.

On the other hand, we saw some who took advantage of the situation. At the time before Katrina hit, gasoline prices were less than $2.00 per gallon. Immediately after the storm came ashore, we saw pictures of a gas station in Georgia selling gas at $5.69 per gallon. This station owner hadn't paid higher prices yet and had no way of knowing just how high a price he would have to pay. He saw an opportunity to make an extra few bucks because of the panic and he took it at the expense of his neighbors. And there were similar accounts of bottled water and other necessary commodities being sold for exorbitant prices.

Those who tried to take advantage of the situation would have done well to read this next Proverb (11:26)—**"He who withholds grain, the people will curse him."** God does not look favorably upon the greedy, especially when their greed results in taking advantage of the suffering of others.

We are called and even commanded in the Bible to give generously and allow God to replenish so we can give even more. This Proverb implies that we must take it even a step further and give generously when circumstances look grim. The implication of withholding the grain has to do with some outside event that is causing a squeeze on the supply. When supplies get squeezed, you can count upon prices going up. The implication in this Proverb is that price gouging is in play. But the lesson of this Proverb is, instead of hanging on to the commodity you possess until the prices get higher and higher, sell and/or give away the commodity as the people have need, regardless of the possible future price. From God's perspective, the economic principle of supply and demand is not a principle we should operate on in times of need.

Those who remain generous even in times of great calamity will be blessed by the people (and by God)—"**but blessing will be on the head of him who sells it.**"

The essential point is for us to be generous even when it may not seem to make practical sense at the time. God is paying strict attention and He will take care of your needs as you take care of the needs of others.

On properly using influence

In the movie *Trading Places*, a wealthy man makes a one-dollar bet with his wealthy brother that he can turn a successful business man into a thief, while, at the same time, turning a con man who lives on the street into a successful business man. His premise was that a man's external environment is the major factor in his character. While I disagree with that last statement, the plot of the movie makes a good illustration for this Proverb—"**Many will seek the favor of a generous man, and every man is a friend to him who gives gifts. All the brothers of a poor man, hate him; how much more do his friends abandon him! He pursues them with words, but they are gone**" (Proverbs 19:6–7).

As the wealthy brother was setting things in motion to win the bet, both of the pawns in this wager immediately saw a change in the way they were treated by those around them. The business man had his assets frozen and was framed for a crime he did not commit. None of his "friends" came to his aid or believed that he had been set up. Meanwhile, our con man was given a terrific job, a fancy house to live in, a luxurious wardrobe, and a hefty bank account. He now had "friends" that he previously didn't even know.

Those who have much can find an audience everywhere they go. Those who have little can't find an audience even when they beg for someone to listen. All of us tend to place a value on what others say based on their perceived level of success. It doesn't necessarily have to be financial success, even though this is the main issue Solomon is discussing, but success in any venture will give you audience with some who would otherwise have no interest in hearing you out.

I have two quick applications from this understanding of this Proverb: First, understand that your level of influence in this world is greatly determined by your success and expertise in any given field or endeavor. Ecclesiastes 9:10 says, "**Whatever your hand finds to do, do it with all your might**." Your first priority as a Christian is to become an expert at handling the Word of God and also apply this to your job, your schooling, your relationships, etc. We are Christ's ambassadors, and, to have the influence we need to make a difference for the Kingdom, we need an audience with people. You will not have that audience if you simply coast through this life, ignoring the impact of a good reputation. You should not make success or expertise your god, but your pursuits should be made with integrity and passion.

Secondly, don't follow the crowd and abuse your influence to treat people poorly. Don't show favoritism to those who have financial well-being, fame, or success. Treat all people with the respect they deserve. God gives each of us the ability to make wealth in varying degrees. Most of the biographies you read about the great missionaries show they had very little in the way of material wealth. Some lived in horrible conditions and went without food for extended periods of time. If you bumped into someone like this on the street, you would never have the opportunity to draw from the well of their spiritual knowledge and experience—because you would most likely judge them by their appearance and apparent lack.

In your quest to discover and attain God's best in your finances, make sure you don't prejudge, use, and then discard people along the way.

Work is important and it is ordained by God. There is more to say on this and related topics, but we'll merge that in later with other components of handling finances God's way.

* * *

TAKE ACTION

Check your attitude about work. Understand the truth that God has ordained work, God has created work, and God has determined that work is good. Begin each workday by thanking God for your job and asking for help to glorify Him in all you do, to be the proper witness and testimony to your superiors and coworkers.

CHAPTER 4

SEIZE THE DAY

M ediocrity. For all the talk of being the best version of you that you can be, for all the self-help books and videos that push us, even for all the advertisements that offer products and services that will supposedly transform us into super humans, our culture incessantly pulls us to mediocrity, and breaking out of that gravitational pull is much harder than you can imagine.

Being mediocre requires nothing beyond average knowledge, average work ethic, average energy, and average initiative. Show up to work on time, do what's expected, and clock out at the end of the day. Go home, eat dinner, watch a bunch of television, and get to sleep at a decent hour, so you can start the average process over again. Feel free to dream of better days but don't take any positive consistent action to draw you toward those dreams.

Make sure that you spend everything you earn, carry credit card debt, have at least one if not two vehicle loans, and refinance your mortgage every five years or so to pull the equity out. Forget the advice to have a sufficient emergency fund and plenty of savings and investments; you'll be kicked out of the ranks of the mediocre if you deviate from the norm. But, since you are reading this book, you are already bucking the system; you are confident that there is a better way and you are resolved to find it.

In this chapter, we will learn a few nuggets of wisdom from Solomon on the vital nature of planning, recognizing, and seizing opportunities; setting priorities; and the dangers and pitfalls of making riches your ultimate goal.

Planning

When my wife and I moved to Colorado in the southern suburbs of Denver, we could see the beauty of the Rocky Mountains, but we had not yet taken a trip to experience them. We had been here for about seven months before taking a few days off for a mountain adventure. I found an available cabin and off we went. It was early November, but the weather was nice, the drive was beautiful, and the cabin was nestled amongst the spruce at the base of many higher mountain peaks—we even had a small pond out front and a mountain stream close by. For a couple of city kids, this was about as close to heaven on earth as we could imagine.

Our first morning at the cabin, we went for a walk down a path heading up into the mountain. As it turned out, this was a small mountain road (although it was only wide enough for one car). We decided to go back to the cabin, get in the car, and see where the road went. We drove slowly for an hour or more, winding our way around the mountain as we climbed, so we could take in all the scenery. The mountain stream I mentioned earlier was running alongside the road and we saw several beaver dams. The rock formations were breathtaking, the trees were pristine, and the snow was glorious. Wait a minute—snow?

We had climbed to the point where we were now driving up a steep mountain road (Did I mention it was only wide enough for one car?) with snow on the ground. It was becoming increasingly difficult to get good traction with my all-weather tires. And oh, by the way, we were driving a 1994 Cadillac Deville! Not exactly the vehicle of choice for navigating a one-lane mountain road with no guard rails in the snow! The thought of now having to back down this snow-packed, narrow, and curved road was, to say the least, frightening.

Well, to state the obvious, God miraculously intervened and we were able to get the car turned around on a snow bank (the only way I can describe it is God literally spun the car around perfectly). The next ten to fifteen minutes was still frightening as we descended far enough to get back on dry ground. We had probably driven fifteen miles or so around that mountain. We were not dressed for the snow and cold (down by the cabin when we left, it was probably in the 50s or better), were down to a quarter tank of gas, and, to top it off, we had no idea where the road was going, and, for some reason, nobody thought cell phone coverage was needed up on a mountain where nobody lived. We were totally unprepared for what we headed into.

I was reminded of this experience with this next Proverb—**"The wisdom of the sensible is to understand his way, but the foolishness of fools is deceit"** (Proverbs 14:8). Reading Solomon's words as often as I have, I see him constantly comparing and contrasting the wise and the foolish. I must say I grow weary of seeing myself in the role of the fool so often—but we all must learn, right? We must learn the way of the wise and we must learn from our times of playing the fool.

Solomon's lesson is for us to take the time needed to look ahead and plan for the future. These plans should always include God (James 4:13–16), but we should plan nonetheless. Some go through life living only for today and leaving tomorrow for tomorrow. On the surface, this may seem to be the way of faith. After all, Jesus said, **"So do not worry about tomorrow, for tomorrow will care for itself. Each day has enough trouble of its own"** (Matthew 6:34). We must all take heed to the words Jesus spoke, but the context of His words were about our propensity to worry. We also must understand the fine line between trusting in God and presuming upon God. Yes, we must live a life of faith, and yes, we must depend upon God's provision on a daily basis, and no, we cannot see what the future holds for us tomorrow. So, letting tomorrow take care of itself is indeed a biblical principle—but, at the same time, God commands that we prepare for tomorrow.

It's a delicate balance—a balance that determines if you fall on the side of the wise or on the side of the foolish. Careful planning that includes consulting God through prayer and through the reading and studying of His Word will help you find and maintain that balance because making wise but flexible plans is critical as well as biblical. So, the next time you have a mountain to climb, find out where the road leads first—and maybe consider driving something with four-wheel drive!

Let's follow up on the importance of including God and His Word in our plans and let's begin with an exercise.

Stop for a moment. Briefly consider how many plans you have made today. Maybe you are like me and use a daily planner or keep a "to-do" list of some sort. These lists can get scary at times in the scope of accomplishing everything you've jotted down, but it only represents a fraction of the plans you make in a given day. In the recesses of your mind, you make hundreds of plans on a moment by moment basis. Your brain reacts and responds to the ever-changing circumstances of your day, shifting and sorting through what you have already written down and making the necessary adjustments. These adjustments aren't always the best course of action, but these plans continue to be made throughout your day—almost unconsciously.

The Bible is clear that we are responsible to make wise plans in many areas of our life. We are to make plans for the future regarding our finances and families. We need to be prepared for the "what-ifs" and emergencies that inevitably spring up, and many other scenarios that we won't take the time to uncover. Making plans is a biblical concept if we allow room for God to change those plans as He sees fit.

The phrase "*let go and let God*" has great application when you are trying to control something that only God can control, but we can actually disobey the Scripture if we take that sentiment too far. We cannot ignore our responsibility in the process. For example, if you find yourself in a financial mess due to your own poor planning and unnecessary spending, you can't simply "*let go and let God.*" Why? Because our disobedience to the financial principles God has given us in His Word is the reason we are usually in the mess. You can pray that God will have mercy and help bail you out, but you can't just "*let go*" and ignore your responsibility.

The point can't be worded any better than what God has already given us in our next Proverb—"**Many plans are in a man's heart, but the counsel of the LORD will stand**" (Proverbs 19:21).

What is the Lord's purpose? That's the big question, right? But it is not a mystery. The Lord's purposes are all written down for us in His Word. His purpose is simply for us to take seriously all that He said. His Word will be fulfilled down to the very last word and syllable. So, when our plans do not match up with what His Word says, can you take a wild guess as to which will prevail?

How, then, do we apply this in a practical way? First, know what His Word says and that only happens by committing ample time to the reading and studying of your Bible on a daily basis—or daily, deeply, and desperately as I often tell my congregation. Then, we need to put into practice everything we learn. Finally, we must make our plans with our Bibles and hearts open. If you keep a daily "to-do" list, how many of you have ever prayed over it before you prioritize your day? How often do you consult God's Word when in the process of making your plans?

If we truly know and understand that the Lord's purposes will prevail, then we will also truly know and understand that it is foolishness to leave Him out of the process—for anything.

Seizing opportunity

A tremendous benefit of having firm, detailed, and God-honoring plans is we will be better prepared to recognize and pounce on opportunity.

The ancient Greeks had a statue called Opportunity sculpted by Lysippus. The statue had winged feet, a great lock of hair coming from his forehead, and was completely bald in the back of his head. The inscription at the base read something like this:

Who made thee? – Lysipus made me.

What is thy name? – My name is Opportunity.

Why dost thou have wings on thy feet? – Because I fly away swiftly.

Why hast thou a forelock? – So anyone can seize me when I come.

Why art thou bald in back? – When I am gone by, none can lay hold of me.

Opportunity is a fleeting thing. We cannot control the timing of when it will come our way, and we cannot keep it and store it away for a more convenient time after it arrives. When opportunity presents itself to you, you have to work on its schedule, not yours. If you delay, more often than not, that particular opportunity will be gone. Opportunity rarely shows up when circumstances are perfect for you to pounce on it, so you must be prepared to make the adjustments in your schedule when possible.

In this next Proverb, Solomon shows us one of the dangers of not taking advantage of opportunity in due season—"**The sluggard does not plow after the autumn, so he begs during the harvest and has nothing**" (Proverbs 20:4).

A lazy person will find every reason known to man to avoid doing what needs to be done. In this instance, it is implied that the sluggard won't work because it is too cold outside. If the weather was perfect, though, you better believe there would be another excuse.

The example of plowing is an excellent illustration. You simply cannot farm on your own schedule. The plowing has to be done at a certain time. The planting has to happen within a small window of time. The harvesting has to happen at a specific time. A farmer can't stay in the farmhouse and wait for perfect conditions during any of these seasons. When the opportunity to do these specific chores presents itself, you had better get busy or you will not have a crop. If you plow and plant too late, your crop will not ripen in time. If you wait too long to harvest, the crop will rot.

You don't have to be a lazy farmer to miss opportunities, though. Taking advantage of opportunity crosses all situations of life—not that we must take advantage of all of them.

Some examples that you might miss: If you have children, don't get so busy with your career and your own life that you miss their childhood. You have one opportunity to raise them right and show them what a mother and a father are supposed to be. If you have a friend who needs a helping hand, don't delay—someone else may step in and receive the blessing while you are still contemplating if you have the time or resources to help. If you are prompted to call a parent, or an old friend, or even a distant relative, get on the phone and do it—you don't know what tomorrow holds for either of you.

If you "miss" the opportunity to save and invest your money, but instead spend it all, you can't go back and make it up. Every dollar you spend is a dollar that is not working on your behalf to secure your future; it is, instead, a dollar that is at work securing someone else's future. The amazing nature of compound interest can and does create millionaires every day, but it requires time; there are no shortcuts and no substitutes for the required time for compound interest to work its magic. So, skipping out on the opportunity to save and invest instead of spending is opportunity forever lost.

When you choose to let opportunity slip by, there are consequences to pay. In our Proverb, the lazy farmer has no food. The lazy parent won't know their children when they are grown and gone. The lazy friend that refuses to help won't have many friends. The lazy relative and/or friend that doesn't call will one day no longer have the ability to call. The lazy saver or investor will be relying on friends, family, and the government to live above the poverty level.

We could all probably benefit from having a picture of the statue that Lysippus sculpted. It would help remind us to take advantage of the opportunities that come our way with urgency, and on a more regular basis.

Another way we are so easily duped into missing out on opportunity is spending too much time with frivolous pursuits—**"He who tills his land will have plenty of food, but he who follows empty pursuits will have poverty in plenty"** (Proverbs 28:19).

I used to own and operate a small lawn and landscape company many years ago in the suburbs of Chicago. Typically, in April and early May, there was a good chance of rain several days each week. The grass would grow like crazy during this part of the season and I had to take advantage of every dry day to keep up. I couldn't depend on the weather always cooperating with my schedule or with whether or not I wanted to take a day off. When the work was there, and the weather was dry, I had no choice but to get out there and cut grass if I wanted an income.

There were times when I did not take advantage of the opportunities. I not only missed the chance for additional billings with my clients but I occasionally lost clients because they had a weekend barbeque with tall grass. In the summer time, we would go through periods of drought and there wasn't any grass growing enough to cut. Those lost additional billings would have come in very handy during these dry times—but the opportunity was lost.

Even though I did not necessarily know this Proverb, and others like it back then, God taught me the principle by allowing me to live it. Take advantage of the time you have.

I once had a ministry to inmates at various federal prisons across the country. I sent them devotions I wrote, written copies of sermons I had preached, and Bible studies from the lessons I taught throughout the week. I also corresponded briefly with them. Each time I received a request in the mail from a new inmate, my first letter back to them encouraged them to take full advantage of the time they have. I tell them that I am not envious of their situation, but that I was envious of the amount of time they had—time to dedicate to the study of God's Word. I encouraged them to consider having a goal of being a Bible scholar by the time their sentence was complete because, once they were released, that time for study would be very difficult, if not impossible, to recapture.

Taking advantage of the time you have is God's recipe for success; purposely squandering the opportunities is God's recipe for disaster. This Proverb is an iron-clad guarantee, not just a possible outcome of your choices. Work hard when the work is there, and you have your needs provided for; slack off when you could be working, and a time will come when you will be living in want.

Priorities

Life is a series of choices. Many of us act as if most choices are already made, and thus we actually do not have a choice in the matter. This is not true, we still have the choice. Let me give you an example of what I mean. Because of the financial obligations we have tied ourselves to (mortgages, car loans, credit card debt, etc.), most people feel they have no choice but to get up on Monday morning and head to their job. Well, that's not true. You still can choose to stay home and risk losing your job, thus risk defaulting on your loans, and thus risk being out on the street so to speak. It's not much of a choice, but it is still a choice, and it is important for us to remember that. Hopefully, by the time we finish this next Proverb, I will be able to help you understand that everything that comes your way is a choice, and that we should make our decisions carefully instead of just letting them be made for us.

"Better is a little with the fear of the LORD than great treasure and turmoil with it" (Proverbs 15:16).

First things first—Solomon is not, by any stretch of the imagination, saying it is better to be poor than to be wealthy. He is also obviously not saying it is better to be wealthy than to be poor. The state of your financial well-being at any point on the spectrum from poverty to riches is not the issue. The context is asking how financial means affect your spiritual life. The point is that your spiritual well-being is far more important to God than your financial well-being. If the size of your bank account determines your relationship with God, you have missed it all. And, as a side note, I say without a doubt those who preach and teach financial prosperity as a *measure* of your spiritual growth are perverting the Scripture!

God is the One who gives us the power to make wealth—and it is His choice! Nothing we do guarantees us wealth. His promise to us is that our needs will be met and that, as we are faithful, we will receive more than we need to share with others. Our problem is we have horribly blurred the line between needs and wants. We don't "need" huge televisions, state of the art smart phones as soon as they hit the market, luxury vehicles, more house than reasonable, and Neiman Marcus clothes, etc. And again, there is nothing intrinsically wrong with having any of these things. The problem lies with when we view these things as needs. Well, I am obviously straying off into a "hot-button" issue with me, so let's get back on point.

The major point is this, if you have to choose between having great wealth (but it comes with turmoil) or having very little financial means (but it comes with peace and a reverential fear of the Lord), then you would be wise to choose the latter. And here is where the choice lies on a more practical level. Most people in our country have made the choice to give away a great portion of their life, meaning they have chosen to have "stuff" in exchange for their time. They have chosen to live life at a breakneck pace to have more "stuff" instead of having more time (having more life). With travel, we put in ten to fourteen hours at our job so we can afford all the "stuff" we buy, and then we store it all away in our homes with the big mortgage. Well, I hope you get the point—and I am as guilty as any of you may be at times.

Understand that you have the choice. You can choose to continue giving away the life you have in order to support a "Keep-up-with-the-Jones" lifestyle; or you can choose to live more simply, and thus live more life with what matters most—your relationship with God and your relationships with those God has placed around you. It is a choice!

The next Proverb continues the lesson on choices and priorities—"**Better is a dish of vegetables where love is than a fattened ox served with hatred**" (Proverbs 15:17).

The Hebrew words used in the first phrase of this Proverb are difficult to translate. Some say vegetables, some say herbs, and some say soup. And, back in Solomon's day, nobody was opposed to eating meat. Regardless of your preference in the types of food you like to consume, the point is this—it is better to choose eating something you really don't like with people you love than to eat your favorite meal with people you are in conflict with.

But even that is not the main issue here. We are again drawn to the choices and priorities we make, choices that lead to living with peace and tranquility or living with strife and turmoil. The previous Proverb dealt with our level of financial status and how the pursuit of "stuff" over the more important spiritual matters brings turmoil instead of peace. This Proverb deals with the same theme—**vegetables** relate to the simple meal of one who does not have much in the way of material possessions and financial means; **a fattened ox** relates to wealth.

Solomon is, again, teaching us that the pursuit of wealth at any cost is not worth the problems that come along with it. Wealth tends to distance you from people who do not have similar bank and investment accounts unless you are very wise in how you use that wealth. Most people do not have the godly character required to treat and use their wealth in a God-pleasing way, so their relationships often suffer.

Let me again make myself clear, there is absolutely nothing wrong with having or even pursuing wealth if it does not consume your thoughts. The lesson here is, when you reach a crossroads, which choice is better? If God blesses you with wealth and you have been given the gift to make even more wealth, then use that gift accordingly. But if you reach a point in time where the pursuit of wealth is affecting your relationships, or you begin to fall into the trap of spending that wealth on the accumulation of "stuff," or you forget God in the process, you have consciously or unconsciously made an unwise choice. And Solomon is saying it is better to give up that wealth and its pursuit for a simpler life that is rich in relationship and ministry. You can absolutely do both but it takes tremendous wisdom from God, and probably accountability to a godly friend to make it work.

The path of having wealth is littered with land mines that Satan has strategically placed along the way, which is why God speaks to the issue of wealth and possessions so abundantly. Be wise in your choices, do not sacrifice that which is important in those choices, then get those charcoals burning (if, like me, you love a good steak).

Your choices and priorities are also better served if you have an ample amount of patience.

Many years ago, I read a book titled *The Art of the Long View*. It wasn't a Christian book; it was a business book that was proposing the concept of looking at everything you do with long-term results in mind, not simply the short-term benefits of a particular decision. For example, a teenager who has just graduated from high school may see the short-term benefit of enjoying college life for four years (while accumulating massive debt). The long view would show that the four-year degree (and massive debt) in our current environment does not typically get you the job and income that a less expensive trade school or apprenticeship would provide with notable exceptions. The short-term benefits of an abundance of entertainment pales in comparison to the long-term benefits of spending those same hours reading and learning to better your life.

Solomon gives us a "long view" look at the ultimate benefit of wisdom—"**The path of life leads upward for the wise that he may keep away from Sheol below**" (Proverbs 15:24).

Ultimate spiritual wisdom leads to salvation. And, while there are many short-term blessings for confessing Jesus as Lord, there are also many hardships and trials that will come your way for naming the name of Christ. Some of these hardships and trials could be avoided if you chose to ignore Christ's call to salvation and lived in accordance with the world. The trials and hardships we face as Christians are designed to bring us into spiritual maturity (James 1:2–4). Apart from the trials, we would never come to full maturity. Apart from being a genuine Christian, we would probably not experience some of the trials.

Short-term thinking says, "Eat, drink, and be merry—don't worry about the consequences of today." The long view understands that every action you take today has a benefit or a consequence tomorrow. I can enjoy eating cookies and cakes and pies and candy today, but the long view says I will gain weight and have poorer health tomorrow. On the other hand, I can discipline myself to eat good, healthy foods today (still satisfying my short-term hunger) and, in the long-term, enjoy more energy and vitality for the length of my days.

Through the years, and still to a great extent today, Christians have faced torture and death for their faith in Jesus Christ. Their tormentors, many times, have given them the option of denouncing Jesus and saving their life or continuing to profess Christ and losing their life. The short view says to save your own skin. The long view echoes the words of Christ—**"He who has found his life will lose it, and he who has lost his life for My sake will find it"** (Matthew 10:39).

The world says Christians are weak. They claim we use Christianity as a crutch. God says it is the only wise choice—those who ignore this choice are not only foolish in the short-term, they can look forward to eternity in a literal hell for the long-term. The so called "weak" Christians have an eternity of unspeakable and indescribable joy in heaven awaiting them. The greatest joys you can imagine on earth are but a momentary and counterfeit benefit compared to the everlasting and true benefits of heaven.

In the context of our pursuit to gain wisdom with our money, the short view says to spend and enjoy today. The long view says you can easily still enjoy today without the extravagant and foolish spending while also setting yourself up for an enjoyable future. The wise path is the long view—but, when you truly understand all the implications, it is actually the best short-term path as well.

Prioritizing and planning out our time is also necessary if we are to maximize our effectiveness in any area of life and will have strong implications in our ability to properly handle our finances.

We are all busy people. Some may be busier than others, but we are all busy. The struggle lies in what we are busy with; how do we prioritize and place value on the activities that can and do fill our days.

I often struggle with knowing if any of my pursuits need to be dropped. Sometimes I feel like I am "stuck" with all of them; sometimes I truly love doing all of them; and I, at times, wonder if I am letting my personal feelings get in the way of God's direction; I wonder if I am allowing human logic and a lack of trust weigh too heavily in my decisions.

Our next Proverb deals with priorities—"**Prepare your work outside and make it ready for yourself in the field; afterwards, then, build your house**" (Proverbs 24:27).

We have a contrast of two important issues: food and housing. Both of these issues are vital in their own right, but both cannot be pursued at the same time; only one is necessary to sustaining life. You must eat to live. Building a house of your own is nice but not necessary.

In my life and in yours, we need to make sure we are doing what is most important. Seek God's help by praying and by studying His Word, then evaluate what is the most important activity you should be involved in. This evaluation should happen on a regular basis and there should always be room for God to change your course.

Working in the field represents what is necessary and building the house represents what you desire. Follow God's priorities and do what is necessary and He will eventually give you the time and resources to do what you desire. Unfortunately, most of us pursue what we desire ahead of what is necessary or what God desires—and that is a prescription for disaster.

Avoid impatience

The allure of riches, when sought after improperly, has destroyed many people throughout history. Some have sought riches improperly by gambling. And although gambling is legal in many places, it is not a proper way to seek riches. Others have sought riches by recklessly speculating in the markets. Speculating (as opposed to investing) in the markets may indeed be legal, but there is a right and a wrong way to go about it. The Bible encourages us to wisely invest our money, but there are many so-called investment vehicles that are not for the wise.

Solomon deals with how we obtain money in this next

Proverb—**"Wealth obtained by fraud dwindles, but the one who gathers by labor increases it"** (Proverbs 13:11).

The term translated as **"obtained by fraud"** means "from vanity." The underlying meaning of the word is that of worthlessness, or that of something that is fleeting or does not last. This same word is used in Proverbs 31:30 where it says, **"Charm is deceitful and beauty is *vain*"**—meaning beauty does not last, or beauty fades away with time. So, the truth Solomon is relating to us is that wealth obtained improperly or by worthless means does not last.

I don't have the statistics handy, but the overwhelming majority of those who obtain wealth by way of a winning lottery ticket, or by an unexpected inheritance, or by cash rewards from lawsuits, etc., find themselves back to the same financial status they had prior to getting this money within a few short years. When wealth is obtained quickly and without doing something tangible to earn it, it **dwindles**.

But the one who gathers by labor increases it. Those who obtain wealth wisely and through hard and honest work will understand what it took to earn it, and thus will understand how to properly treat the money God has blessed them with. They know how to care for, invest, and put money to good, God-ordained uses. And, as they prove their worth in being a good steward, as opposed to a spendthrift, God blesses them by allowing this fortune to grow and be circulated.

Don't be in a hurry to be rich. Put in the time and the effort to obtain wealth in God's timing, in God's plan, and by God's principles.

Allow me to share from my own foolishness in being in a hurry to get rich.

In the late '80s, I dabbled in the harrowing world of investing in the futures market. This is one of the riskiest ways you could invest your money—if you can even call it investing. Some say investing in futures and commodities is just as risky as walking into a casino. And, although I have never gambled in a casino, I think, for many who get involved in this type of investing, it is legalized gambling to them—I know it felt that way to me.

When I first got involved in this market, I got "lucky" almost immediately. I invested in coffee and, unbeknownst to me, a drought had just begun in Brazil. Within a few short weeks, I was making $3,000 a day and, of course, I thought I was a genius investor. I thought to myself, *How easy is this?* After I had quickly amassed $40,000 or $50,000 in a month or so (more than I was making annually at my job), I decided to become broker and do this for a living. I had found the short cut to riches I had been looking for.

Solomon's words in yet another Proverb could have done me some good back then if I was looking—"**Wisdom is in the presence of one who has understanding, but the eyes of a fool are on the ends of the earth**" (Proverbs 17:24).

After I had quit my job and obtained my broker's license, I thought I had found the elusive "Easy Street." All was right with the world in July of 1987. Then, reality set in. It rained in Brazil, wiping out most of my gains, and other commodities I had foolishly jumped into went south as well. I was having trouble getting clients to invest through me since I had no track record, and my wife was pregnant with our second son and was about to take a year off work to raise him. Our son was born in September, and, in October of 1987, the stock market crashed (some of you may remember a day that was called *Black Monday* by Wall Street).

Hard lessons were learned over the next few years, yet I had had a taste of quick money, almost a gambler's rush of sorts, and I still occasionally got involved in "get-rich-quick" schemes and multilevel marketing companies of questionable reputation. There are many honest and legitimate companies out there that have chosen multilevel marketing as their way of growing the business, but, for me, the attraction was easy money. I was always looking for the next big thing—**the eyes of a fool are on the ends of the earth**.

The way of wisdom is always best. But wisdom does not come overnight. And wisdom is not as flashy as the blinding light of potential quick riches. When it comes to investing your money, the slow and steady approach is actually the fastest way to lasting riches, and God's wisdom encourages us to be shrewd with investing. Yet, hardly any of us actually handle our money according to God's principles. Instead of keeping our eyes glued on wisdom, we do let our eyes wander to what may be a short-cut or a so-called sure thing.

It took me more than twenty years to fully learn the lessons God had to teach me back in 1987. I trust this journey into my past will be of some help to you. Always choose God's wisdom, especially when it comes to money; it tends to quickly disappear, which is the lesson in this next Proverb.

"Do not weary yourself to gain wealth, cease from your consideration of it. When you set your eyes on it, it is gone. For wealth certainly makes itself wings like an eagle that flies toward the heavens" (Proverbs 23:4–5).

Often, in a Bible study I teach, one of the participants would exclaim, *"I needed to hear and study this material a long time ago."* How often do we come across a verse, a passage, or a principle in God's Word that has that impact on us? We read and understand something God has always wanted to teach us, if we would have simply taken the time, and we immediately can go back to a time when that information would have helped us avoid a lot of mistakes and pain. I had one of those moments the first time I really read this Proverb, as indicated in the story above.

What are the lessons to be learned in this Proverb?

First, we have already seen that the accumulation of wealth is not inherently a bad thing. God does not condemn riches and He does not exalt poverty. But, conversely, God also does not condemn poverty and exalt riches. The amount of money you have is not the issue. God is only concerned with your attitude about riches and how you handle what you have been given—regardless of the amount.

Second, when we do have an ample amount of material wealth (and an ample amount is different for every one of us), we need to apply wisdom like never before. We need to search the Scriptures for every piece of advice and commands God has given regarding the use of that wealth and our attitude toward it.

Third, we must understand that wealth can disappear overnight even if we are being wise. Markets collapse, currencies are devalued, wars break out, thieves steal, and catastrophes happen. During the fall of the Soviet Union, people were using the paper money they had as fuel for fires to keep warm—their currency had become worthless.

I have long since stopped trying to get rich. I still have much to learn and apply from my continuing study of God's plan for finances and material possessions, but I can tell you that the less I focus on riches and the more I focus on gaining wisdom, the more wealth (little by little) God has entrusted to my care.

I have one last thought on the theme of this chapter—returning to the excellent wife, or Proverbs 31 woman, for more wisdom.

Proverbs 31:16–18 says, **"She considers a field and buys it; from her earnings she plants a vineyard. She girds herself with strength and makes her arms strong. She senses that her gain is good; her lamp does not go out at night."**

Each of us has the same exact twenty-four hours every day. You can spend those hours any way you choose but you can only spend them once. It is like having a bank account that receives a deposit of $24 at the stroke of midnight for you to do with as you please (if it gets you a little more into the illustration, you have my permission to make that $24,000); but, at 11:59 the following night, whatever wasn't used disappears forever.

In our current earthly human condition, time is always marching on. Nobody has the power to stop time, add time, or subtract time; the seconds tick away relentlessly. We have deadlines to meet, decisions to make, and appointments to keep, all of which are constrained in one way or another by time.

Solomon teaches us in the Book of Ecclesiastes that there is a time and a season for everything, including rest and relaxation. But, sometimes, our rest and relaxation can reach the point of laziness and waste, and wasting time does not make the grade in any context of the Scripture.

The key, according to this passage, for not wasting time is wise and discerning preparation. She is prepared by the fact that she has taken the time to consider this field (this investment). This was not a spur-of-the-moment, walking through the mall and having a sweater beckon you to come in, type of decision. She has carefully weighed the pros and cons and negotiated a fair price; she has planned out a use for the field that will allow her investment to come back to her in due time. She is prepared because she has earnings in store that she has saved to purchase the field with cash, and thus not becoming a slave to the lender and wasting precious resources on interest payments.

She is prepared by keeping herself in good physical condition to be able to handle the rigors of tending a vineyard well, thus, insuring a good crop and yield on her investment of money and time. Her preparation also gives her strength of mind and attitude to be ready for the task ahead, not shrinking back from the hard work. She is prepared by continuing to plan and schedule her days even if it requires burning the midnight oil.

In all of this, she is content and satisfied that her purchase was indeed a very good one.

Compare these activities with the normal day-to-day routines of most today. Boredom and depression rule the day. Television and the Internet consume ungodly amounts of time. We can find ourselves ever busy but never accomplishing anything of value and worth.

What's the difference? Preparation and the will to tackle your plans; an attitude of choosing to use your twenty-four hours productively; a will to turn off the TV, turn off the computer, and even unplug the phone if necessary to focus on making wise and discerning plans, and to get on with the tasks at hand.

No one said this was going to be easy, but the rewards will be well worth it.

* * *

TAKE ACTION

What does excellence mean to you? After you determine the best definition of excellence, be brutally honest on how often and how diligently you pursue excellence. Would the people you know and even outside observers consider you to be excellent in all you do? With each chore, job, ministry, responsibility, or pursuit, measure your performance against what is excellent.

CHAPTER 5

WHAT'S IN IT FOR ME?

You may be asking at this point, "*If I go through the hard work of study and application of the principles found in the Book of Proverbs, am I guaranteed success?*" Or, as the title of this chapter suggests, "*What's in it for me?*"

God has always promised blessing when we observe His Word. The entire premise of the Book of Proverbs is essentially "Do this and get that" whether the positive rewards or the negative consequences. The wisdom of Solomon, and of the other writers included in this book of Scripture, has given us an instruction manual for success. If you could go back and study in detail the successes and failures you have experienced, you could find a principle in Proverbs that correlates to every one of them. Your successes were the result of following a principle or principles and your failures were the result of violating a principle or principles in this amazing book even if you were ignorant of what you were following or violating.

So, are you guaranteed success if you put in the hours of study and then adhere to what you learn? The answer is yes, but the problem is we typically pick and choose what we are going to adhere to instead of wholeheartedly studying and applying all of it.

So, if you are asking, "What's in it for me?" the answer is fully dependent upon the resolve, or lack thereof, you have in truly studying and then applying ALL OF IT.

We will look at God's provision and blessing along with several aspects of the results we can expect when heeding the wisdom found in Proverbs. Let's start with the Provider.

God's blessing and provision

Quick—if I were to ask you to make a list of people you know or are acquainted with who were blessed, who comes to mind? Is it the family that is struggling to make ends meet? Is it the person who is currently in the hospital? Or is it the family that just bought a new car, or the person who gives the largest offering at church? If you are like most Christians, you will tend to equate the blessing of the Lord with material possessions and financial status.

We see this attitude even in the oldest book of the Bible, the Book of Job. Job was a wealthy man. He was "**the greatest of all the men of the east**" according to Job 1:3. Even Satan looked at the wealth of Job in determining how blessed Job was—"**You have blessed the work of his hands, and his possessions have increased in the land**" (Job 1:10b).

When God allows Satan to take everything away from Job, including his health, Job's friends gather around him to discuss his dire situation.

For days, Job's friends try to convince him that his sin is the reason that he no longer had the "blessing" of God. Their attitude was that the blessing of God was only manifest in material things, so the fact that all of Job's wealth and material possessions were now gone meant that Job was no longer blessed. Something Job did or didn't do has caused the blessing of the Lord to be withdrawn from him—human effort. Job refutes this notion throughout much of the book.

We see this same attitude even among the Apostles. The Apostles ask Jesus a question in John 9:1–2, "**As He passed by, He saw a man blind from birth. And His disciples asked Him, 'Rabbi, who sinned, this man or his parents, that he would be born blind?'**" The Apostles simply assumed the blessing of God was not upon this blind man just because he was blind. Again, assuming that some form of human effort was lacking in this person's character or the character of his parents. Jesus also refutes this notion.

Solomon says, **"It is the blessing of the LORD that makes rich"** (10:22a). Now, before you say this verse affirms Job's friends and the Apostles, understand that the underlying Hebrew word is in the sense of a gift, not something that was earned. Also, being materially rich is not the only way a person is indeed rich in blessing from the Lord. In Matthew 5:3–12, we have the Beatitudes. Money or material possessions is not mentioned once, yet Christ proclaims God's blessing on those who have these essential attitudes.

The next phrase will also help us in our understanding—**"and He adds no sorrow to it"** (10:22b). The word translated here as "**sorrow**" can also be translated as "labor." If you take this interpretation, we see that human effort has nothing to do with the blessing of the Lord in this sense—it is all from God as He pleases.

So, everything you possess, everything you are able to do, and even the status of your physical health (whether good or bad in your eyes) is a blessing from the Lord— and these blessings indeed make you rich. Don't assume material wealth is the only way you are rich, and thus the only way you are blessed of the Lord.

As we look into the many actions that we can take to improve and add to these blessings, do not miss this vital truth that God is the Provider at all times. And sometimes, His generous provision is yet another layer of His amazing grace—not anything we could possibly earn.

Allow me to digress for a moment to, again, admonish you to be mindful of becoming obsessed with riches, or even with whatever you consider to be a comfortable existence when it comes to money. We can easily lose the right perspective and have our focus distracted from what is truly important.

In the early years of the church that God allowed me to be the founding pastor, I did a series of sermons aimed at keeping our focus where it belonged. We often tend to ride the wave of ministry and get distracted by the scenery along the way. At the time of this sermon series, our church was looking at possibly purchasing the building we met in, or a piece of land to build on. And, while in most cases in our country, it is important for us to have a permanent place to meet, the purpose of our church is not to be focused on buildings and land. Our primary focus must be on loving God, loving people, being His witnesses, and making disciples. It is amazingly easy for a church to lose this focus if they are not intentional in maintaining it.

It is also amazingly easy for us as individuals to lose our focus. I can lose my focus walking from one room to the next. There are so many distractions in our lives, and it is only increasing every day. Solomon has one of the "big" distractions listed in the first half of our Proverb—**"Riches do not profit in the day of wrath"** (11:4a).

The big distraction that takes more Christians and non-Christians alike off focus is money. Most people obsess over money for the majority of their lives. It doesn't matter if you have very little or you have more than you can ever spend, money is on most people's minds more than any other issue. If you could tally the minutes each day of the issues that cross your mind, you would vividly see that money most likely dominated your thoughts.

On the **day of wrath**, the balance of our checking account won't matter. Money is obviously necessary in the culture in which we live, but it won't be going with us when our time is up. The size of your portfolio and the accumulation of the stuff you own does not and will not impress God. And the fact that you stress out over money does not please God.

Jesus says, **"Do not worry then, saying, 'What will we eat?' or 'What will we drink?' or 'What will we wear for clothing?' For the Gentiles eagerly seek all these things; for your heavenly Father knows that you need all these things. But seek first His kingdom and His righteousness, and all these things will be added to you"** (Matthew 6:31–33). This passage clearly tells us where our focus must be even when there is "more month left at the end of the money"—our focus must be on the Kingdom of God.

Our job is to pursue God's Kingdom (reading, studying, and applying God's Word to our life, loving God, loving others, spreading the gospel, and making disciples) and let God take care of our needs, and we already touched on the difference between needs and wants. Letting God take care of needs does not mean ignoring our responsibilities to work and earn an income, it is simply adjusting our focus away from money being our god. We must shift our paradigm to one that keeps our eyes fixed on Jesus, and then we must reshift our paradigm as often as necessary when our attitude about money tries to, again, take precedence.

That is why Solomon can then say, "**but righteousness delivers from death**" (11:4b). The term **death**, in this instance, means eternal death not physical death. Godly living, which includes a proper view of money, leads us on the path to life everlasting. Jesus confirms this thought in the passage we just read—"**For the Gentiles eagerly seek all these things**" with Gentiles referring to unbelievers.

Money is the most talked about topic in the whole Bible because we are so easily enticed by all that it can bring us. Keep your focus on the more important, eternal issues. For when our focus, attitude, and paradigm is directed properly, God's provision also includes protection.

Many years ago, we had two golden retrievers in our home. Charlie was about seven to eight years older and about fifty to sixty pounds heavier than Daisy, so, when it came to meal time, Charlie would usually bully his way into more than his fair share. To ensure that Daisy was getting enough food, I would, at times, send Charlie outside and feed Daisy alone, and I would also slip her some extra scraps when Charlie wasn't looking. As Daisy grew, she learned to fend for herself quite well, but, initially, she needed some assistance. I had to oversee both dogs to balance things out when necessary.

God looks out for us in this way and beyond. He protects us and provides for us when the need arises, but He also allows us to fend for ourselves if we choose to ignore His help. The Scripture is full of verses that deal with how God helps and blesses the humble and how He thwarts and curses the proud. One of those verses is the next Proverb in our study: **"The LORD will tear down the house of the proud, but He will establish the boundary of the widow"** (15:25).

Pride derails more Christians from the path of godliness than any issue. Pride keeps you from coming to God for help when times are tough, thus sometimes extending those tough times. Pride keeps you from praising God when times are good, thus shortening those good times. Pride keeps you from forgiving those who have wronged you, thus developing and harboring bitterness in your soul. Pride makes you susceptible to materialism, trying to keep up with your friends and neighbors, thus causing many to face financial ruin. Pride puts your trust in your financial means and your own devices, thus causing you to fall into the sin of idolatry. And, if you are a nonbeliever, the sin of pride is the main factor in your refusal to confess Jesus as Lord.

Pride also is evidenced by impatience. Jeremiah 42:7 says, **"Now at the end of ten days the word of the LORD came to Jeremiah."** One of the most dedicated prophets of God went to Him for some answers and God waited ten days before responding. We stress out and do things our own way after ten minutes, if that. Learn patience or God will teach it to you—and it won't always be pretty.

God will only allow pride in your life for so long before He comes in to destroy it. On the other hand, those who are humble can expect the Lord's protection in due time. Again, borrowing from the life of Jeremiah—prior to the Babylonians laying waste to Jerusalem but while the armies of Babylon were gathering outside the city walls, God tells Jeremiah to purchase some property. Knowing that impending doom is imminent, Jeremiah found some very eager sellers. After the city was leveled and the surviving residents were carried away into captivity, the Babylonian captors allowed Jeremiah the choice of coming to Babylon or staying behind in Judah. God protected Jeremiah and his new property.

So, we can do things on our own and face the inevitable consequences of our choices apart from God, or we can trust in Him and receive His blessing and protection. Seems like a pretty easy choice, although admittedly not always easy to do. Work on defeating your pride at every opportunity—the effort will be well worth it.

Keep things real

I have a group of Christian friends whom I became acquainted with during the time my wife and I owned and operated a small Christian bookstore. Besides being big fans of Christian music (several of these guys worked in that industry in one form or another), we also shared a love for sports. One of these friends invited me to join them in a fantasy football league. It's called fantasy football because I'm not really an owner of a professional sports team—I just get to pretend that I am. In my own eyes, I am in charge of a team I have assembled to compete for the championship (which, unfortunately, is pretty rare).

This next Proverb deals with a certain aspect of a fantasy world—"**The rich man is wise in his own eyes, but the poor who has understanding sees through him**" (28:11).

Many people who accumulate great wealth attribute their fortune to their own wisdom, knowledge, abilities, and talent; and, for some, you could make a pretty strong case from a strictly human perspective. Contrary to popular opinion, most wealthy people have worked hard to reach the level of income and wealth they have obtained; obviously, some acquired their wealth through inheritance, lotteries, and other less rigorous means. Regardless of how their wealth was accumulated, unless they are students of the Bible, they all probably believe they had a great deal to do with where they are at. They are definitely wise in their own eyes.

Deuteronomy 8:18 makes it clear that the Lord is the one who gives people the power to make wealth. And just so there is no misunderstanding, we are talking about those who come by their wealth through legitimate means. God does not give power to mafia kingpins, drug lords, and thieves to make wealth (God always settles accounts). For those who came by their wealth in legitimate ways, the ability to make that wealth came from the Lord. They still had to take the necessary steps to see their wealth come into being; it says God gives the power to *make* wealth, so we must do what is necessary in accordance with the principles of the Scripture. So, from a purely humanistic point of view, the wealthy may truly believe it was their wisdom that brought the wealth but, from a biblical point of view, without God, the wealth would have never been there.

This is what Solomon is trying to get across when he speaks of the **poor who has understanding** being able to see through the rich man who **is wise in his own eyes**. The key is not that this man is poor but that he has a measure of understanding referring to God and His Word.

Sadly, some would argue and teach that, if the poor man truly had understanding, he would not be poor based on the notion that God wants us all to be prosperous in a material way. That would have to be a discussion for another time, but God wrote this Proverb, and, all throughout the Book of Proverbs, the context of a wise man or a man of understanding is one who is wise or understanding in the ways of God, and a man or woman's level of material prosperity has absolutely no bearing on wisdom and understanding in the context of this Proverb.

The lesson we should glean from this Proverb is not whether or not God wants you to be wealthy, but that everything you have comes from God. And a man or woman of understanding will recognize this and attribute it all to God. We cannot ever fall into the trap of entering the world of fantasy by thinking our wisdom and knowledge is the reason for our wealth.

We have a part in wisely handling what God entrusts to each of us, but we live in a fantasy world if we think our wisdom is the primary reason for any success.

Doesn't God want me to be rich?

When it comes to Scripture, we need to always believe what we read (in the proper context) instead of reading what we believe. This is much more difficult than it sounds because all of us have a set of values and beliefs that have influenced us our entire lives. If you grew up in a church of any kind, there are lasting influences from the teachings of that church that are still ingrained within today. Many of those teachings are probably in line with the Scripture and need to be continued. Some, unfortunately, are only dogmas of a denomination or of a particular teacher/preacher that have very weak support from the Scripture, if any at all.

A few of the teachings I grew up with fall into the latter category. When we started the church I currently pastor, we determined to do so with no preconceived denominational teachings or doctrines that could not be undeniably supported in God's Word. I had to retrain my mind to view the Bible with fresh eyes and to make sure everything I believed was completely backed up by the principles of the Scripture in its full and proper context—not just what I was comfortable with. I will admit that I have a long way to go in my understanding of the Scripture, but I will also say that God has opened my eyes to some things and increased my understanding exponentially in these years as a pastor.

This next Proverb touches on the dangers of being firm in a wrong belief—**"An arrogant man stirs up strife"** (28:25a); and it also touches on one of the biblical teachings that is dismissed by some, abused by others, and misunderstood by most—**"but he who trusts in the Lord will prosper"** (28:25b).

Let's begin with the topic of spiritual arrogance before attempting to understand what prosperity truly means.

Spiritual arrogance is counterproductive in the church. I will go so far as to say it is a sin and is probably the primary contributing factor in most, if not all, church splits. Spiritual arrogance reveals itself in those who believe they have reached a different level of maturity in their Christian existence, and those who have not reached that level simply do not measure up. There is an impatience in the hearts of the spiritually arrogant. They have a great deal of trouble waiting for others to "catch up."

The problem is that, if you have 100 genuine believers in the same room, you are going to have 100 slightly to greatly different levels of spiritual maturity. Our relationship with Christ and our growth in Christ is very personal and will vary greatly as the Holy Spirit works in our unique lives. My relationship with Christ is not the exact same as yours, and yours is not the exact same as the next person's. Praise God, He cares for us and treats us (and created us) as unique individuals, and He reveals Himself to us in unique ways as we are ready to receive. God doesn't view one of us at "level 3," if you will, with any more love and care than someone at "level 10." When we attempt to drag someone from level 3 to level 10 for the sake of fulfilling our own personal agenda, we are attempting to bypass all that needs to be learned at levels 4–9. We are essentially saying, *"God, you're taking too long with so-and-so, so I'm going to have to step in and take over,"* or worse yet, *"I'm going to ignore this person until they measure up."*

This kind of spiritual arrogance stirs up strife. As a pastor, I have to search for balance all the time. Yes, I want to continue to mature in my faith and my understanding each and every day, and I desire that those under my influence are advancing in their Christian walk as well, but I am not responsible for dragging and forcing others to keep up with me—I am not the standard! Also, as the pastor, I am not called to leave my brothers and sisters behind when they are not growing as quickly as I would like. 1 Thessalonians 5:12–15 makes it clear that we are to deal with all levels of Christian maturity with complete patience.

Your relationship with Christ and your spiritual growth is a personal and intimate walk with the Lord. It should be growing day by day and your brothers and sisters in Christ should be lovingly encouraging you all along the way, but it is personal between you and the Lord. Don't be guilty of becoming spiritually arrogant by allowing your pride to tell you that you are better than others because you have arrived at a different level or because the Holy Spirit has granted you a particular gift—remember that you too were once at level 1, 2, and 3. Don't be guilty of stirring up strife.

Now, let me wade into the dangerous waters of determining what the Scripture means by the oft abused word—prosperity. If we enhance what the Bible says, or add some of our own views and experiences, entire movements can be born based only partially upon what God's Word says.

One of the many dangers of this practice is many will dismiss what the Bible says elsewhere because it doesn't fit the careless teaching made by a handful.

The last half of this Proverb is one of these issues that has been carelessly taught in many circles—**he who trusts in the Lord will prosper**.

Some of you reading this have already made up your mind regarding what prosperity means. I implore you specifically, and the rest of you in general, to examine why you believe what you believe. If we do not do the hard work of proper study, we will often dismiss what God has said in the context of how and why He said it.

It's easy to blame "the other side" for abusing the Scripture simply because we like what pastor so-and-so teaches or what the TV evangelist says, but have we taken the time to personally study through what the Bible teaches? Have we allowed the Holy Spirit to shape our understanding instead of allowing what "feels" right or what appeals to our flesh to make that determination?

My point in this discussion is not to rile anyone up—both sides are already firmly entrenched in their positions without my comments. I am also not asking you to throw away all of your convictions and beliefs without good cause. My goal is to somehow ease and eliminate the animosity that exists between the different evangelical denominations and churches, and thus the animosity between brothers and sisters in Christ. Because, when this animosity exists, we tend to close our minds, and thus miss what God's Word is saying to us. And we also then present a very confusing picture of the church to a lost and dying world, which hinders our ability to witness.

My theology is not 100% accurate and your theology is not 100% accurate; only God's theology is 100% accurate. The Bible is the source for our theology and, the instant we add to it, or read into it, or take something away from it, our theology is immediately flawed—because it is now OUR theology and not God's.

Beloved, all of us desperately need to be so immersed in God's Word that we will recognize error through the prompting of the Holy Spirit, not just because of what we have been taught by any particular preacher, teacher, or denomination. Always, always, always go to the Source and confirm the truth of the matter through the whole of the Scripture and through the leading of the Holy Spirit—don't just rely on what you think is the truth.

In the past, I never read certain authors or listened to certain preachers and teachers if they did not fit in with my theology. I now look for the good and discard the bad with any author I read or any preacher or teacher I listen to. Sometimes I find fault with some aspects of what is being written or spoken, but also find tremendous truth or principle in other aspects. At the same time, I used to take everything certain preachers/teachers said as gospel truth, but I have found that some of *his* or *her* theology is not supported very well, if at all, in the Scripture. Everything must be weighed against the truth and purity of God's Word. We must be like the Christians from Berea who compared everything Paul and Silas said against the Scriptures (Can you imagine questioning whether Paul and Silas were teaching biblically?).

The last part of our current Proverb again states, "**he who trusts in the Lord will prosper.**" It doesn't say he might prosper, or he could prosper, it says he **will** prosper. Statements like this in the Scripture cause many to go off the deep end on both sides of the pool. Those who believe God wants all of us to be wealthy jump all over verses like this and those who don't believe that premise ignore verses like this or attempt to alter what it means. Both extremes fit the bill of adding to or taking away from the Scripture, which is a horrible sin.

The Hebrew word translated as "**prosper**" in this Proverb literally means "to be fat" or "to cause to grow fat." In the culture in which this was written, fatness was a sign of wealth. In many ways, you could say the same thing today. In our American ideology, we may not consider ourselves to be prosperous unless we have no debt, no worries, and no restrictions on our spending, but, by the standards and conditions of 90%–95% of the rest of the world, the poverty level of the United States falls into the category of prosperity. Much of the world calls us "fat" Americans—which applies literally and figuratively.

The word is used and translated in several other ways as well. The beloved and often quoted 23rd Psalm uses the same Hebrew word when it says, "**You have anointed my head with oil.**" The word translated as "**anointed**" is the exact same Hebrew word used in our Proverb—you have "fattened" my head with oil or "prospered" my head with oil doesn't quite have the same ring to it, but you hopefully get the message. God prospers His obedient children in many ways.

With the nation of Israel, God promised to not only supply the needs of His people but that He would go beyond just their needs if they fully obeyed His Word. He also gave them a grave warning that, in their prosperity, there would be a great tendency to forget who supplied the abundance (Deuteronomy 31:20) and that would lead to judgment, curses, and want. But the same principle from our Proverb is present with the promises to Israel—trust in the Lord and obey God's Word, and you will be made fat or prosperous.

In Psalm 1:3, speaking about the person who obeys and meditates on God's Word, the psalmist says, "**And in whatever he does he prospers.**" The Hebrew word the Psalmist chose is different than in our Proverb but has a similar meaning. Literally the word is defined "to succeed" but another explanation of the meaning of this Hebrew word is worth considering: "*God alone grants true success; He gives prosperity to those who obey His laws and decrees, to those who fervently seek Him and to those who pray for mercy and grace.*"

So, why is prosperity, as related in the Scripture, such a controversial subject? Why do some shun the idea completely while others embrace it to the point of believing something is terribly wrong if you are not prosperous? And then, what about those in the middle who think promises of prosperity sounds too good to be true but secretly hope there is some truth to the concept and wonder how to get in on the deal? And, does prosperity only mean money and possessions? And, if so, are you going to tell me that ALL Christians in poverty-stricken parts of the earth are sinfully disobedient or lacking in faith to the point where they do not qualify for prosperity?

These are difficult questions to say the least—questions I am not sure I will be able to sufficiently answer.

There are eighty-nine variations of nine different Hebrew words that have been translated as prosper, prosperous, prospered, or prosperity—along with several other uses of the Hebrew words translated differently like "**anoint**" as we saw in Psalm 23. The New Testament is surprisingly less generous in the use of the term. There is only one Greek word used and it is only used four times in all (three verses).

The Greek word can be defined as, "to get along well," "prosper," "succeed," or "gain." The word carries the implication that God is the source of the prosperity or success. The *Theological Dictionary of the New Testament* (considered by most scholars to be the gold standard in translating the Greek language used in the Scripture) says this concerning the Greek word: "*This rare term means 'to lead on a good path,' 'to guide well,' 'to bring on to the right path.'*" The related Greek words overwhelmingly focus on the sense of being on the right road, path, way, or course. To sum it up, the emphasis is on following the course God has for your life—whether or not that means financial success cannot be dogmatically claimed based solely upon this Greek word and its usage. Let's look at the four uses with the italics being mine.

- Romans 1:10 – "**if perhaps now at last by the will of God I may** *succeed* **in coming to you.**"
- 1 Corinthians 16:2 – "**On the first day of every week each one of you is to put aside and save, as he may** *prosper,* **so that no collection is made when I come.**"
- 3 John 2 – "**Beloved, I pray that in all respects you may** *prosper* **and be in good health, just as your soul** *prospers.*"

The Old Testament clearly ties prosperity with obedience to God's Word. The New Testament greatly implies the same with the strong emphasis of being on the right path or course for your life. In both instances financial gain can be an underlying meaning but is not necessarily the only or even best meaning. The terms seem more so to be leaning toward the aspect of being successful in all you do in accordance to the direction God has for your life—again, financial gain can definitely be a part of this but does not have to be for the Scripture to be fulfilled.

Scripture is clear that God desires that His children are prosperous (I believe, in every sense of the word), and willing obedience to God's Word is the key regardless of how the prosperity is manifest in your life.

I am quite sure that those of you who were firmly entrenched in your belief of prosperity (on either side) prior to this study are still there—just be sure not to close your mind so securely that you miss some truths of the Scripture. For the rest of you, I trust this brought some clarity to the topic as opposed to muddying the waters even further. Regardless of where you were or where you are now, remember to be obedient to all that God's Word teaches, and then give God the glory and credit for whatever measure of prosperity you experience.

In whatever manner you view prosperity and how that relates to your spirituality, there is a Proverb that is difficult to explain away; but we must keep the undeniable context of accumulating God's wisdom at the forefront of our minds while considering what Solomon has to say.

"I love those who love me; and those who diligently seek me will find me. Riches and honor are with me, enduring wealth and righteousness. My fruit is better than gold, even pure gold, and my yield better than choicest silver. I walk in the way of righteousness, in the midst of the paths of justice, to endow those who love me with wealth, that I may fill their treasuries" (8:17–21).

There is a lot to unpack in these verses but the essence is those who love wisdom, who diligently search for and seek wisdom, who understand that the pursuit and accumulation of wisdom is far greater than the accumulation of riches, who accept and apply that wisdom will result in living righteously and justly—those who have this as their honest goal will, as a side benefit, also set themselves up for riches, honor, enduring wealth, and wealth that will fill your treasuries.

This is vital in our understanding and application of this portion of Proverbs: the focal point is searching for, accumulating, and loving God's wisdom. If your gaze is on the "side benefit" or riches and wealth that will fill a treasury, you've missed the context and cannot possibly claim the side benefit.

That's a tall order. How can we essentially forget or set aside such a promise in the material realm, and have a laser focus on only obtaining God's wisdom, allowing the visions of riches and wealth to only appear as God examines our hearts and determines that we are capable of handling such? To a certain extent, this passage is suggesting that, only when we don't care about obtaining riches and are instead only concerned about obtaining God's wisdom, that riches will come.

I am convinced this lofty idea can only be reached through the power of the Holy Spirit working mightily within us. In our humanness, selfish desires relentlessly invade our thoughts and intrude on the best of motives. We'll even justify and rationalize how generous and charitable we would be if such riches were bestowed upon us. Multiple times I have had people tell me, "If I win the lottery, you can count on 10% going to the church." To which I often ask, "Are you giving 10% now?" Silence or stammering follows.

When the Apostle Paul writes about the daily routine of crucifying our flesh, this is the essence of what he means. Apart from the intervention of the Holy Spirit and the daily renewing of our minds through the power of the Scripture and pleading to God in prayer, we are innately selfish to the core. So, if the "side benefit" of our Proverb is scintillatingly dancing in your mind right now, there's work to be done.

The beginning point is developing a genuine love for God's wisdom, and you cannot merely wish this desire into existence. While it won't hurt, a sticky note on your mirror reminding you to love God's wisdom won't get the results you desire. The only tried and true way to develop an enduring love for God's wisdom is to immerse yourself in it, which means ample time spent every day absorbing the Scripture.

There are numerous methods of reading and studying the Scripture, but developing a genuine love for God's Word requires a resolve and commitment that escapes most of us. This often involves a radical shift in priorities and a major adjustment in the delegation of our use of time. Three hours of television each night and a ten-minute devotional reading doesn't even qualify as flirting with God's wisdom, let alone loving it. Think radical and major.

I discovered a Bible reading program many years ago that was developed by a university professor by the name of Dr. Grant Horner (do an online search). As I began using this system, I got hooked. I made a few adjustments to Dr. Horner's system and then relabeled it as the "Ridiculous Bible Reading Plan" to distribute and promote at my church. I labeled it as "Ridiculous" because, for most Christians, it is ridiculous to read ten chapters of the Bible per day. That being said, I have known many who get so hooked on this style of reading that they choose to read twenty chapters instead—it becomes that addicting.

It is not reading ten chapters at a time in one book of the Bible, but instead you are reading one chapter each day from ten separate lists of books of the Bible (again, do an Internet search for Professor Horner's Bible reading plan for the details). And guess what? The Book of Proverbs is the only book of the Bible in list #7, meaning you will be reading a chapter of Proverbs every day. Solomon will be downloading his wisdom into your brain every day as well as Moses, David, one of the prophets, Matthew, Mark, Luke, John, the Apostle Paul, Peter, and the other inspired writers of Scripture! Every day, you will be getting the absolute best possible wisdom and instruction enhanced by the Holy Spirit's divine illumination. You cannot help but experience a passionate love for God's Word ever growing.

Do the "side benefits" of Proverbs 8:17–21 magically appear? It all depends on your attitude and outlook and how deeply your desire for God's wisdom and His wisdom alone is. But I can promise that your focus will change dramatically, and I guarantee that verse 19, **"My fruit is better than gold, even pure gold, and my yield better than choicest silver,"** will come alive in your heart. And, when the side benefit does make its appearance, God will have molded and shaped and equipped and transformed your heart and mind to handle wealth that could fill a treasury.

Solomon has a similar theme in another Proverb, if not worded in such a manner to elicit dreams of riches in our head, but the theme of commitment is still front and center—**"Commit your works to the Lord and your plans will be established"** (16:3).

Have you ever really committed yourself to anything? I mean truly and wholly committed yourself to a particular plan of action or course of life; the type of commitment that gives you a singleness of purpose or defines everything else that is you. Is there a unifying principle in which all the decisions of your life can be weighed against, or a guiding light that shows you the path you should take when your direction gets lost in a fog?

There is a fine line between being open and flexible in following the Lord's purposes and making your own plans and following them. We must learn to maintain the delicate balance of living out our Christian life as if everything depended upon the Lord while, at the same time, living out our Christian lives as if everything depended upon us. While that may seem like a paradox, God never gives us a mandate or a principle to follow that He will not also give us everything we need to accomplish it.

That balance is displayed beautifully in this last Proverb for this chapter.

I must admit most of us struggle with this balance. Many well-meaning, committed Christians have problems with the day-to-day issues they face. They are like a piece of driftwood being carried by the current and the waves. One moment they are up and the next they are down. They allow the circumstances of the moment to determine their attitudes, and they allow these winds and storms to steal their focus away from their God-given purpose.

The key to avoiding this roller-coaster ride of emotions and feelings is to commit your work to the Lord. In the Hebrew, this literally means to roll all of your business upon God like you would roll a heavy stone over to someone else to carry for you. We must intentionally and specifically roll our works and our burdens and our busy minds and our worries over to the Lord. To do this takes tremendous effort on our part. We spend our lives spinning our wheels in hurrying over here and hurrying over there. We run from one place to another. We try something today and, when the results we desire don't come, we try something different tomorrow. And this applies to those of us who are hurrying and running and trying for the sake of the church and the sake of the gospel—but this is not a picture of true commitment to the Lord. This is a picture of thinking a frantic pace equals progress, of relying on your own self-imposed time schedule and course of action.

When God gives you a purpose and a plan for your life, you must commit yourself to the study of His Word and to the leading of His Spirit and to the discipline of patience. The more we try to push God's plans into happening now, the more we are pushing God out of the way and assuming control.

A friend of mine once confessed to me that he has to get up off the throne daily and allow God to reassume His rightful place. Another friend has told me how we must rest in God like a little child climbing up into his or her daddy's lap. But, just like that little child is too restless to stay in his daddy's lap for very long, we have the same tendency to jump out of God's lap and get about the business of hurrying God along.

When we do let God back on the throne and when we do rest in our Father's lap, we will discover the true meaning of commitment (and contentment), and then your plans will succeed. There is tremendous peace in this great truth. Relax. God is still in control and He knows best. Yes, we must have a sense of urgency in proclaiming the gospel message, but that doesn't give us an excuse to not wait on Him and to not rest in Him. Our busyness and anxiousness accomplish nothing but exhaustion. Our plans are pointless apart from God, which is the primary reason most of us go from one financial emergency to another. Our plans cannot be established apart from committing our works and our ways to the Lord; and our financial plans are rarely committed to the Lord.

* * *

TAKE ACTION

Write down what your expectations are for your finances over the next year, three years, and ten years. If you are expecting the blessing of God in these goals, what are you doing now and what will you be doing from this point on that makes you expect God's help? Make the necessary changes and commitments in your daily routine that will bring your actions in line with your expectations.

CHAPTER 6

THE PURSUIT

The pursuit of getting our financial life in order is ripe with opportunities to lose focus. Developing the discipline of focus is vital. Without it, you can destroy years of hard work, or even a lifetime of denying the whims of the moment to save and invest. Focus is the key.

One of the great challenges we face in the "electronic age" is the discipline of focus. We have such a glut of information coming at us at such tremendous speed that we lose focus and spend untold hours chasing the trivial or getting riled up about any number of topics without any constructive action to make positive change.

The Scripture is full of admonitions to "set your mind on..." "fix your eyes on..." and the like, which teaches us to FOCUS. We can't completely ignore current events or the unending drama of people you care for and love, but we can develop habits to help us focus on that which is truly important.

Give yourself permission to let the world go on without you for at least a few hours each day. Believe me, all the angst and drama will still be there when you return if you have conditioned yourself to enjoy that kind of thing. During those two to three hours, turn everything off, or unplug as they say, and FOCUS on those things in your life that are truly and genuinely important.

If you are constantly wishing you better understood the Scripture, devote an ample portion of your focus time to the reading and study of the Scripture. If you have always wanted to write a book, give your mind and talents the focused time to get started. If you truly desire to take control of your finances, then, beyond reading this book, you must continue to study and then implement the wisdom of the Scripture. If you have a relationship that needs attention, you guessed it, use those hours to work on it.

Stop letting social media, the endless emails, text messages, television, and the like to rule and control your life. You have a limited number of days—don't waste too many of them on that which is trivial and nonessential.

In this chapter, we will survey the wisdom of Solomon to help us in avoiding the many pitfalls that can, and often do, destroy your finances. We will consider our motives, impatience, greed, and tempering the lottery mentality.

Check your motives

I can remember a time, as a young deacon in the church I was raised in, when an influential and wealthy businessman attended our services one Sunday. I can recall discussing with a few other deacons and staff members what a tremendous asset he would be for our church. We were all excited that this man attended a service at our church. I also remember a lady who faithfully attended our church, but she was on welfare, had some mental problems, was loud and obnoxious at times, and smelled strongly of cigarettes. Some of the leaders in the church tried to figure out ways to move this lady into someone else's Sunday school class because they didn't want to deal with her in their class. Looking back, I can't believe that God put up with us as a church for this blatant sin on our part—on both fronts.

It is an unfortunate fact that Christians join the world in often treating people differently depending upon their station in society, their level of financial means, and even the color of their skin. Solomon states this fact in the first of two Proverbs, and then points out the sin in the second—**"The poor is hated even by his neighbor, but those who love the rich are many. He who despises his neighbor sins, but happy is he who is gracious to the poor"** (14:20–21).

James tackles this very issue in his letter—**"My brethren, do not hold your faith in our glorious Lord Jesus Christ with an attitude of personal favoritism. For if a man comes into your assembly with a gold ring and dressed in fine clothes, and there also comes in a poor man with dirty clothes, and you pay special attention to the one who is wearing fine clothes, and say, 'You sit here in a good place,' and you say to the poor man, 'You stand over there, or sit down by my footstool,' have you not made distinctions among yourselves, and become judges with evil motives?"** (James 2:1–4)

What indeed are our motives when we cozy up to someone who is wealthy and, at the same time, ignore or mistreat someone who is poor? While there are some very generous wealthy people in this world, the majority are weary of the attention they receive from those who are really only interested in their money. Yet, we still have this evil lurking within us to show favor to the wealthy on the miniscule chance they may throw a few coins our way. We meet someone who even appears to be wealthy and we, at times, fall over backwards trying to make them feel special.

Mike Tyson was a heavyweight champion boxer for many years. He was also a convicted felon. During his heyday, he had "friends" around him all the time, living off the wealth he created because of his boxing prowess. When the money ran out and Mr. Tyson owed millions, all but a few of his so-called "friends" abandoned him.

We can almost expect behavior like this in the world, but this kind of behavior in the church cannot be tolerated. The Bible is clear that it is the Lord who adds people to the church. When we treat someone poorly because of the condition of their clothes, or their prior reputation, or their lack of means to put something in the offering plate, it is tantamount to us telling the Lord, "*We don't need this one God.*" How dare we!

Better for us to be blessed by God for accepting them as they are and helping them with any needs they may have. The plain truth is many of us struggle with treating all people with equal kindness. Solomon tells us the plain truth is that we sin when we show partiality like this. We cannot allow the allure of riches to shape our attitude toward others, and we also cannot allow such to direct our actions.

As I continue to "mature," I question things more often. One of the things I question quite often are the meanings of phrases that I've heard through the years. I usually understand what the phrases mean, but I wonder where they came from. Here's one that very vaguely connects to our next Proverb (and I mean very vaguely): "*Don't look a gift horse in the mouth.*" My first thought is, why would you look any horse in the mouth? So, I did a little research.

As horses age, their teeth become longer and more protruding. Wise and grizzled horse traders could pretty much tell how old a horse was by examining its teeth. So, by examining the teeth of a horse that was given to you as a gift, you would be insulting the giver of the gift by publicly questioning just how good of a gift this was.

Well, outside of the fact that our Proverb has the word **gift** in it and the phrase we examined does as well, there really is not much connection or application (I told you, it was very vague), but it maybe helps illustrate slightly. So, Solomon makes the statement—"**A man's gift makes room for him and brings him before great men**" (18:16).

This Proverb simply makes a true statement. It does not condemn giving gifts nor does it encourage giving gifts, it simply states a fact—leaving the implications for us to consider on both sides of the issue.

If you are giving a gift, the application would be one of examining your motives. Now, most of us are guilty at times of giving a gift to bribe the receiver of the gift. I can't speak for the ladies, but the floral industry pretty much survives off the bribes of husbands and boyfriends trying to make up for something we've done wrong or overlooked. In that case, we obviously do have a motive, but the motive is a worthy one—peace in the relationship. Now, this is not to say that this is the only reason we buy flowers for our ladies, but, even when we have done no wrong, there is a motive.

This was obviously a harmless example, but you get the point. There are many Proverbs that deal with the bad side of making bribes, but this Proverb is making the implication that there is a time and a place for giving a gift if it will help accomplish a worthy goal.

If you are on the receiving side of a gift, this Proverb is implying that you may want to examine the motive behind the gift. We must be careful here—it is not my desire to turn you into a cynic. I don't want you questioning the giver of every gift you receive, but, if it is unusual to receive a gift from this person, or the gift is of much too high a value, you may want to see if there are strings attached before accepting the gift—but, of course, you don't want to look a gift horse in the mouth (I knew I could get it in here).

But there's more wisdom to consider in gift giving.

Motive is the driving force behind most every decision we make, the good we do, and even the evil we do. Every time you do anything, there is a reason. More often than not, due to our sin nature and the constant battle with our flesh, there is a self-serving benefit somewhere in the background or the foreground that motivates our actions.

We eat for the benefit of satisfying our hunger. We eat chocolate cake for the benefit of ... well, it's chocolate cake! We watch TV for the benefit of being entertained. We pick and choose our friends because we are comfortable with them and they bring us joy. We avoid making friends with others because we are not comfortable with them. The clothes we buy, the homes we live in, the cars we drive, the churches we attend, and the books we read are all governed by our motives.

Some motives are genuinely pure and good but almost all have at least a twinge of self in the mix. It is our nature to desire a benefit from everything we do.

I once did battle with a woodpecker that was trying to take over my hummingbird feeders, and intermittently trying to take some chunks out of my cedar-sided house. It was a beautiful bird, but I cannot seem to get through to that little bird brain that I don't want him or her pecking on my house. And I will never get it through his or her brain because we call them woodpeckers for a reason—they peck wood. It's their nature. Unless there is a way to transform this bird's nature, he or she will always peck wood.

Our mortal bodies (in which we are temporarily trapped) are similar to woodpeckers. Our flesh is selfish. Apart from any other external influence, our flesh will always choose to do what is beneficial for itself at the time. It is our fallen sinful nature and, as long as we are on this earth, the Spirit within us will be constantly engaged in battle with the flesh (Galatians 5:16–26). Because of this, we have to constantly check our motives.

This next Proverb again addresses this issue—**"He who oppresses the poor to make more for himself or who gives to the rich, will only come to poverty"** (22:16).

Solomon warns us that, when our motives are governed by our flesh, we will fail. The benefit we are hoping for will eventually vanish; the promises of Satan are all smokescreens and illusions. If our motives are influenced by our selfishness, we will be like the fool in the desert who sees a mirage and ends up drinking sand.

Constantly check and examine your motives, for they can be wrong and/or influence you poorly. Improper motives may lead you to ignoring rules and laws, or to take advantage of others.

This next Proverb deals with playing by the rules and not taking unfair advantage of people—**"Do not move the ancient boundary or go into the fields of the fatherless"** (23:10).

In ancient times, they did not have county records and surveys that marked the boundaries of a piece of property. Instead, they primarily would have a pile of rocks or some sort of stake in the ground at each corner of the property. Since there were no specific records kept of the exact locations of these boundaries, unsavory landowners habitually moved these boundaries to their benefit. They especially took advantage of the helpless—widows and orphans who did not have the wealth or the manpower to protect their borders.

Even if someone were to seemingly get away with taking advantage of others, God is watching—**"For their Redeemer is strong; He will plead their case against you"** (23:11).

While most of us may not view ourselves as land barons whose appetite for more and more cannot seem to be satisfied, we still must be careful to not violate the principle being taught here—don't take advantage of others and obey the rules that are in place. Because, whenever we break the rules, we are truly breaking God's rules as outlined in His Word. And God is strong, and His justice is true and right and exact. I don't believe any of us really want to find ourselves with God opposing us.

I want it now!

Most of us are an impatient lot. We have been raised in a culture that does not understand how to wait for anything. We want, and usually get, instant meals, instant credit, instant access, etc. We are a culture that stands in front of the microwave with arms folded and toe tapping, mumbling, "C'mon!"

This expectation of instant results has led to all manner of problems in our society. We expect a pill to eliminate the fat and pounds that we spent years accumulating with poor eating habits and lack of exercise. Young people and athletes expect a pill or an injection to build up their muscles instead of long hours in the gym. We expect credit cards to fulfill our desires instead of working, saving, and budgeting to obtain the items we desire. And worst of all, Christians expect a twenty-minute sermon once a week will give them a thorough knowledge of God's Word.

The folly of impatience, unrealistic expectations, or hastiness is the point Solomon wishes to get across to us in our next Proverb—**"Do not go out hastily to argue your case; otherwise, what will you do in the end, when your neighbor humiliates you?"** (25:8)

The implication that Solomon makes is that a hasty rush to judgment will backfire on you. The picture that is painted here is one making a quick and faulty conclusion and then publicly accusing his or her neighbor of the crime. In the end, the neighbor was not guilty, and the accuser was put to shame. So, not only was this person injured in some way by the initial injustice, they get the privilege of adding shame to their problems.

I was once a witness in a court case. The prosecuting attorney was adamant that the defendant was guilty and called him a liar in front of the jury. When the verdict came back as not guilty, the attorney was visibly embarrassed and humiliated. I assume this attorney thought there was enough evidence to prove guilt, but there wasn't (and rightfully so in my opinion).

The application is to simply slow down. Look at all of the facts. What is the end result you are looking for? If your goal is to lose weight, examine what caused the excess weight and then make the necessary changes to eliminate this cause—and that's not going to be found in a bottle of pills. If you want a stronger, leaner body, then find the right exercise program for you and get busy—knowing in advance that this is a new weekly habit for the long haul, not just a month or two. If you desire to make a purchase, take the time to plan and budget and save until you can pay cash for the item. If you desire your savings and investments to grow, forget about the get-rich-quick schemes and follow the principles of the Scripture. If you feel wronged by someone, make sure you get all the facts before jumping to a conclusion.

And give the microwave a break; it's cooking your food as fast as it can.

Bribery and greed

At the church I was raised in, we were attempting to sell a piece of adjoining property that we did not need. The money we could get for the property was sorely needed to alleviate debt and free up more money for ministry. Seemed simple enough to those of us on the board of the church. Seven years later, we finally were able to sell the property. The sale was not held up because we didn't have any potential buyers. No, the sale of the property was primarily held up because the planning and zoning commissioner was waiting for us to pay him off to get the proper red tape pushed through. When we refused, our plans kept getting tied up with an unending stream of issues that kept us off the agenda for the planning commission meetings. And when we did get on the agenda, there was always something else we needed to do before approval.

Bribes are a way of life for many people who are in positions of authority. Everybody knows the game, and most turn their head and pretend it isn't happening. And those who don't play the game end up waiting seven years for something that shouldn't take seven weeks. But just because everybody else is playing the game, it doesn't mean that God approves—"**He who profits illicitly troubles his own house, but he who hates bribes will live**" (15:27).

From the Hebrew, the first phrase of this Proverb could be translated as, "He who is greedy for gain … " The person who is greedy to hit the jackpot will generally do just about anything to cash in, which is why bribes are commonplace. If there were no people who accepted bribes, they would eventually stop. Salesman will sometimes get the big sale, not because they did the best job of selling and had the right product to sell, but because they promised the largest kickback. Many politicians get elected into office because they have some wealthy supporters who finance their campaign—and then want something in return when they assume the power of the office.

I think Exodus 23:8 states the insidiousness of bribes very well—"**You shall not take a bribe, for a bribe blinds the clear-sighted and subverts the cause of the just.**" When bribes are offered and accepted, someone who is doing things right and honorable gets cheated.

I would assume that most, if not all, of us have never solicited or accepted a bribe in the way we are discussing—but let's bring it down a notch to see if this Proverb does apply to us in even a small way. We must examine our own lives and see if any of the activities we take part in constitute bribery—even if no money is changing hands. The definition of a bribe is being persuaded to do something that you otherwise would not do because of the personal gain you will receive.

With that definition of bribery, we need to be careful of our motives at all times. Our good deeds should come from a genuine heart of love for others. If we receive a benefit from doing the good deed, so be it, as long as that is not your motivation. If your motivation is to receive praise and attention from others, then you are guilty of accepting a bribe in doing the good deed. Inherently, there is nothing wrong with receiving praise and attention for doing good, again, as long as that is not your motivation and reason for doing the good.

We are told that first impressions are very important. I heard a report on the radio recently that most of the people in corporate America who do the hiring for the companies in which they work make that decision in the first ten seconds of an interview. You can hardly say hello in ten seconds. So, I guess in this regard, first impressions really are very important.

At other times, first impressions can be deceiving. If you were to just give this next Proverb a casual reading, it may appear that Solomon is promoting the virtues of bribery—**"A bribe is a charm in the sight of its owner; wherever he turns, he prospers"** (17:8). But if we dig a little deeper, we will find out what is really being said.

Let me start by giving you an example from the movie *Mickey Blue Eyes*. In the movie, Michael, an auctioneer of fine art, falls in love with Gina Vitale, a school teacher. Gina's family is mafia—a fact she has hidden from Michael. Michael finally convinces Gina to marry him and he is introduced to the "family." Unbeknownst to him, the family does a few favors for Michael that helps his business. A bribe here and a bribe there and everything begins to run smoothly. Michael is now expected to do some favors in return. In this movie, being a comedy, all the wheels fall off and away we go.

Why do people engage in the practice of bribery? Because it works … at first. And, all of us engage in this practice quite often. *"Honey, if you'll paint the house this weekend, I'll make your favorite dinner."* Or maybe, *"Son, if you will get your chores done by lunch time, I'll take you fishing this afternoon.*" Bribery does not have to involve laundering money or receiving a kickback. Just like most anything in this world, there are varying degrees of severity, but it's still bribery.

Solomon does not condemn the practice of bribery in this Proverb, but he does not commend it either. But the implication is that the one who engages in bribery can become deceived into believing that he or she can always get anything they want as long as the bribe is strong enough. You can be tricked into thinking that bribery is the key that will unlock any door. What we must consider from this implication is the motivation behind making the bribe and the price you will have to pay in the long run.

In our movie example, Michael was asked to sell a hideous painting at his next auction in return for the favors he received. Another person was planted in the audience to pay an outrageous sum for the painting and, when the price was then paid, illegally obtained money was laundered.

Which brings us to the point I wish to make—bribery can seem harmless when it comes to motivating someone to do some chores, but it can easily turn into something much more insidious. If you are bribing your children to do chores that should be done out of simple obedience, you are conditioning them to only obey when there is an incentive for them to do so. And, if something happens that does not allow you to "pay up" in a timely manner, more bribes are needed, and, just like in the movie, the wheels can fall off.

Don't get involved in the bribery game in the more traditional sense of the word, but also be careful that you are not getting involved in the bribery game even in a subtle sense, and take even more care when you are having struggles with your finances.

There seems to be nothing that occupies a person's mind more than financial troubles. When you are behind in your bills with no real prospect of getting ahead, or when you've lost your job or had your income curtailed in some way, it is very difficult to find a moment when your mind is not swimming with worry and concern about money.

I have been in situations before, and still—if I am not diligent in accepting and believing what the Scripture says—find myself struggling at times today with thoughts of concern over money. I pray until I simply can't imagine any other ways to pray about it, and I put my mind to work to make sure I haven't missed anything. I examine my life to see if there is any unconfessed sin, and I do my level best to turn it completely over to God, but it's still there weighing on my mind and destroying my effectiveness in any other endeavor. How do you concentrate on your job, or on your ministry, or on helping others, or on any other pursuit or responsibility when you can't eliminate financial concerns from your mind?

When I first read this next Proverb—**"A man with an evil eye hastens after wealth and does not know that want will come upon him"** (28:22)—I thought maybe it was speaking to me in some way. Maybe I was hastening after wealth and was thus bringing want upon myself instead, but then I realized I had missed the key phrase in this Proverb—**"A man with an evil eye."** What does that mean? Who is **"A man with an evil eye"**?

The underlying sense of the Hebrew wording means an unethical person, with a strong implication of also being miserly. This is a person who is pursuing riches with no regard for how he or she obtains it. This is someone who takes unethical shortcuts, who always takes from the penny tray but never contributes, who cheats on their taxes, who takes advantage of people and situations when it has the potential to line his or her pockets, etc. Solomon is not telling us that wealth is bad or even that pursuing wealth is inherently bad, he is just warning us of the dangers of pursuing wealth unethically and with a miserly spirit—and the danger is instead of achieving wealth you will achieve poverty.

The Scripture is clear that God is the one who distributes the power to get wealth. God gives us directions for how to receive it, how to use it, what kind of attitude to have about it, and—if we disobey His directions—how to lose it. The Bible also adds a seeming paradox of telling us to be content with whatever situation you face regarding your finances. How can God show us the path to prosperity in His Word and, at the same time, teach us to be content where we are right now?

The passages of the Scripture that show us the path to prosperity always have the condition of strict obedience to His Word—and most people (not all) who are in dire financial straits are there because they have violated one or more of God's commands in the use of money and/ or have violated any number of other principles in God's Word.

The primary struggle I want to continue with is how financial woes weigh you down and dominate your thoughts, attitude, and spirit. And, for that, I want to take you to Philippians 4:5b–7—"**The Lord is near. Be anxious for nothing, but in everything by prayer and supplication with thanksgiving let your requests be made known to God. And the peace of God, which surpasses all comprehension, will guard your hearts and your minds in Christ Jesus.**"

When financial worries consume you, the primary ingredient that is lacking in your life is peace. Peace and worry cannot coexist. Peace and depression cannot coexist. Peace and panic cannot coexist. God tells us how to reacquire peace when times are tough. But He not only tells us how to reacquire peace, He tells us how to acquire the peace of God which surpasses all comprehension. Let me ask you a question: Do you think God ever worries? Do you believe God ever goes into a panic about His financial condition? Does God ever walk the halls of heaven wringing His hands and mumbling, "What am I going to do now?"

It's pretty ridiculous to consider God in such a way. God is in control of all things and He has the answer for every issue you are facing now or will face in the future. His timing in providing for you is perfect. His prescription for what ails you is precise and exact. And His peace is available to you right now regardless of your circumstances. Your life and mine should be carefree, which is the implication when Paul says, "**Be anxious for nothing.**" The word anxious means full of care; and when you are focused on your financial troubles, you are indeed full of care. And, quite honestly, since we are told in the Bible to be anxious for nothing, when we are carrying that load of care, we are disobeying God's Word—and that is sin.

So, repent of your worry, take every last concern to God in prayer as often as you need to, be thankful that God hears you and is watching over you at all times, and allow the peace of God to overwhelm you and to guard your heart and your mind in Christ Jesus. And do you know why you can do this? Because this tremendous passage of the Scripture begins with the truth that **the Lord is near**.

Because the Lord is near, you can be anxious for nothing. Because the Lord is near, you can take absolutely everything to God in prayer. Because the Lord is near, you can be thankful in all things. Because the Lord is near, you can experience the peace of God that surpasses all comprehension. Because the Lord is near, your heart and mind can be guarded in Christ Jesus.

Beloved, I do not always know the answer to why God, at times, seems slow to bail us out of our problems. I do know it is impossible to fully mature in Christ without experiencing trials and tribulations according to James 1:2–4. I also know this—the Lord is near, and He has full knowledge of your situation and monitors you and your life every second of every day. You will survive, and, according to God's Word, help is on the way in the Lord's perfect timing. His mercies are new every morning and His peace is as close as your next prayer.

So, pray for help in pursuing His way in your finances, and pray for the courage and resolve to follow His precepts in all things, which will pave the way for His divine and supernatural peace.

There is another important aspect to avoiding greed and having the proper perspective with our finances—it impedes our ability to destroy selfishness.

I took an economics course at a local junior college while still in my twenties. The course took us through some of the history of modern economic thought and introduced us to the basic components that drive an economy. Most of what I learned made sense, meaning I could at least see the logic behind why certain inputs or causes in an economy brought about certain outputs or effects. But some of the concepts and theories did not make sense to me; I couldn't logically make the connections. Economics is not an exact science; what worked in the 1980s will not necessarily work today because of political influence and pressure, along with many other fluctuating factors.

God's economics typically defy human logic. God says, the more you give away, the more you receive; the more you keep and hoard, the more you lose. And we have an example of that in yet another Proverb—"**He who gives to the poor will never want, but he who shuts his eyes will have many curses**" (28:27).

Giving to the poor is a concept that is encouraged all throughout the Scripture. God even saw fit to make it a part of His Law that was handed down through Moses. One of the three Old Testament tithes was designated primarily to provide for the poor (and yes, there were three tithes, for those who wish to somehow mandate the tithe in the church today—a tithe is great measuring stick for New Covenant giving, but not a mandate, which is a discussion for another time). The corners of the fields were not to be harvested but left for the poor to take. Any produce that was dropped during harvest was to be left on the ground for the poor to gather. Every seventh year, the fields were to be left alone and whatever grew on its own that year was for the poor. Many other provisions were made and many other examples of giving to the poor are scattered throughout God's Word.

The implication from our Proverb goes beyond what we see on the surface. The sense is that those who are habitually benevolent will not be lacking in the necessities of life nor the luxuries of life. The stingy will have multiple curses come down on them and will not escape their punishment because God stands behind His Word. God's economy, unlike any human-based economy, is an exact science so to speak; specific input always produces specific output. God always keeps His Word and will always reward those who give from their heart and will always curse those who hoard.

The Scripture is clear that our giving must be from the heart—it's an attitude. Giving for the sole purpose of receiving will not produce the same results as giving from a compassionate heart. Giving out of compulsion will not produce the same results as giving with a grateful, cheerful, and willingly obedient heart.

If you struggle with giving as you know you should, start by making it a habit to pray that God will give you His heart and compassion for people. If you are sincere in this kind of prayer, God will begin to allow you to see the need through His eyes, and you will then begin to experience the promises and blessings of God as He intended. And your heart and attitude will be divinely transformed.

Get rich slow

In America, the majority of our population has a "lottery" mentality. What I mean by that is most people expect something for nothing. We hear stories of people hitting it big in the lottery, or winning a substantial amount of money on some TV game show, or getting a huge settlement in a lawsuit because the coffee you spilled on yourself was "too hot." We have all had dreams of hitting it big someday. The problem is we dream of hitting it big without putting in the necessary time and effort. We want a money tree in our backyard that we can pick from anytime we want.

In these next four Proverbs, Solomon wants us to gain the wisdom of "Cause and Effect." There are tremendous benefits available to us if we will simply understand that benefits come to us only when we do the things necessary to gain them in the slow process of gaining them. You can't walk up to the personnel manager of a company and ask them to give you a paid vacation and free health insurance, but you don't want to work for that company. The benefits go only to those who work for the company.

If you want things to change in your life, then YOU need to change. If you continue to do what you have always done, you will continue to get the results you have always gotten. If you want different results, you will need to take different actions.

Cause and Effect #1 – "**Ill-gotten gains do not profit, but righteousness delivers from death**" (10:2). The gap between a lottery mentality and gaining wealth through unlawful means is not as wide as some might think. When we are always thinking about gaining wealth in some big way, we almost begin to think that we deserve it—and when it doesn't come or come as quickly as we think is right, we begin to take advantage of "opportunities" to benefit our desired lifestyle. You may take a few shortcuts to start. When you seemingly get away with that, you go a little further until, one day, you are doing things you would have never dreamed of doing. But these gains do not last, and all the money in the world cannot buy you more time when the end of your life comes. Choose **righteousness** as your "Cause."

Cause and Effect #2 – "**The LORD will not allow the righteous to hunger, but He will reject the craving of the wicked**" (10:3). There are times when some of us experience being somewhat destitute. Whether it is because of the loss of a job, an unforeseen emergency, or something else, we can experience not knowing how we are going to continue to put food on the table. God's promise to the **righteous** is they will not **hunger** to any extreme. The "Cause" is godly living, the "Effect" is always enough food to live on. On the other hand, those who live **wicked** lives will never have enough. They will always want more regardless of how much they already have.

For a moment, let's look at worldly success. There have been many studies done on the characteristics of successful men and women in this country. These men and women come from all manner of backgrounds and some of these studies exclude those who had inherited substantial wealth. One of the characteristics that were common among most who have succeeded (at least from the world's point of view) is their attention to what is important. They are very frugal with their expenditures—not cheap, but frugal. They do not spend money on unnecessary things or even necessary things if it is not important to have at that moment.

Let me give you a small example of how I did not have this attitude of frugalness in my business pursuits. I once owned a small lawn and landscape business. When I started the business, even before I had mowed a single lawn, I spent money to have some nice business cards, to get the right stationary, and on and on. Not necessarily wrong things, but, in my financial condition, things that were not necessary to start generating an income in the business. Instead of focusing on what was necessary and important—generating an income—I was focused on looking good.

Solomon has two more "Cause and Effect" Proverbs for us that pertain to this "lottery" mentality we are focusing on.

Cause and Effect #3 – "**Poor is he who works with a negligent hand, but the hand of the diligent makes rich**" (10:4). This verse speaks to us of having a proper work ethic in our lives. It also implies that we not only work hard but we also work wisely. We must have understanding concerning our work. We should study the work we have to be the best we can possibly be. Those who work hard and work wisely will be rewarded well; those who are lazy when it comes to work will receive the reward of poverty.

Cause and Effect #4 – "**He who gathers in the summer is a son who acts wisely, but he who sleeps in the harvest is a son who acts shamefully**" (10:5). Here, we have the wisdom of taking advantage of opportunity, which we have studied previously. The primary work in which Solomon writes is that of a farmer or farm hand. There are certain times of the year in the farming business when you simply do not have enough hours in the day to complete all that needs to be done. During these times, you must take advantage of every hour you have. Work when the opportunity is here to work. Don't presume upon God by thinking the opportunity will last or be here again tomorrow.

We cannot have a lottery mentality. We must focus on what is important, we must work hard and work smart, and we must take advantage of the opportunities that God gives in due season.

As almost always, Solomon has more to say on a subject in various other Proverbs, which is the case with the lottery mentality.

Something for nothing. This seems to be the desire of most people. Our society and culture promote this fantasy through state lotteries, casinos popping up everywhere, and mailings telling you "*You may have just won $10,000,000.*" Many of America's youth leave school and expect the world to be handed to them—they want to sit at home and play video games, sleep until noon, and get a fat paycheck at the end of the week. The concept of working hard for forty hours per week is totally foreign to a whole generation. And this can be said about many of the adults as well.

Something for nothing is not God's way for us to live our lives—even though God has given each of us something for nothing. The redeemed of the Lord enjoys the gift of God's salvation by grace alone for nothing in return. We all enjoy the blessings of God's provision for nothing in return. We all enjoy the love of God for nothing in return—and on and on it goes. But even though God continually gives and gives to us when we do not deserve anything, He requires us to put forth an effort during our earthly existence. Work is ordained by God and laziness is despised by God.

God ordained work in Genesis 2:15 when He "**took the man and put him into the garden of Eden to cultivate it and keep it**" (and this was before sin came into the world). By Genesis 3:19, man's work grew harder due to the effects of sin. In Exodus 20:9, God establishes the six-day work week (somehow, we have decided that a five-day work week is better). You will find verses ordaining and even commanding mankind to work in Leviticus, Deuteronomy, Joshua, Judges, Ruth, 1 and 2 Samuel, 1 and 2 Chronicles, Ezra, Nehemiah, Job, Psalms, Proverbs, Ecclesiastes, Isaiah, Ezekiel, Hosea, Habakkuk, Haggai, Matthew, Mark, Luke, John, Acts, Romans, 1 and 2 Corinthians, Philippians, Ephesians, 1 and 2 Thessalonians, 1 and 2 Timothy, Philemon, James, 1 and 2 Peter, 1 John, and I am sure you can find it in every other book of the Bible. There is no way around it—we must work.

Solomon approaches this issue of work from two different perspectives in these next two Proverbs. First, he deals with the aspect of working to eat and then he contrasts the sin of coveting with the godly command to be productive.

Working to eat – "**He who tills his land will have plenty of bread, but he who pursues worthless things lacks sense**" (12:11). The premise is that you must work if you want to eat. The contrast is that a fool will waste his time in leisure and laying around the house instead of going out and working. Make good use of your time—work hard when work is available.

Coveting vs. producing – **"The wicked man desires the booty of evil men, but the root of the righteous yields fruit"** (12:12). The wicked sits around coveting the deceptive gains of other wicked people. They spend their time desiring what they do not have and scheming ways in which they can obtain it (as long as it doesn't require hard work). The godly make better use of their time by being productive. They put their hands to work accomplishing something of value to them and to their employer with their time. They don't covet what they don't have, they work to obtain what they don't have, whether it is to obtain an education, or to obtain a new house—it doesn't matter. They understand that work is required to obtain anything of value, and they get about the business of working hard to obtain and to obey God's command.

Something for nothing just doesn't work. Wanting it all immediately just doesn't work. This leads me to what I'll call the sprinter's mentality.

At summer youth camp one year, we had a mini Olympics for the sports competition and activities. There were team sports of basketball, softball, and volleyball and there were a host of individual competitions, including weightlifting, and many track-and-field events. In the latter, one of the competitions was the 4×4 relay. A one-mile distance was measured off and each of the four members of the team would run one quarter of that mile after the baton was passed to him. I was a good player on the basketball, softball, and volleyball teams, but I have never been known for the fleetness of my feet.

For some reason (I think somebody got hurt), I was enlisted to be a member of the 4×4 relay team. They put me as the third leg of the team, so I waited patiently as I watched the first two members of our team start the race and promptly give us a big lead. When the baton was passed to me, I took off as fast as my tree-trunk legs would carry me. By the time I reached the fourth member of our team, the big lead we had was gone—the other teams made up the deficit because they had real sprinters for their third leg. Fortunately for our team, our anchor (the last sprinter of the four) was the fastest kid at camp and he cruised to the finish line ahead of the others for the victory.

I found out that day what I had already suspected—I am not a sprinter. I had decent endurance back then, so I could run for long distances and long periods of time, but I was not a good sprinter.

The last Proverb in this chapter, deals with the sprinter mentality —**"He who loves pleasure will become a poor man; he who loves wine and oil will not become rich"** (21:17).

Most people in our culture have the sprinter mindset when it comes to life. We want everything our parents had and more, but instead of taking the twenty to thirty years it took our parents to achieve their station in life, we want it now! We spend much more than we earn by misusing credit and assuming we will always have a job and the ability to pay off these loans. We beg our doctors to medicate our problems away instead of making the necessary life changes to alleviate the stresses that cause many of the physical ailments we are afflicted with. We eat fast food, processed food, fat-laden food, preserved food, and any other form of food that is quick and easy because we refuse to take the time to prepare healthy and nutritious meals.

This mindset spills over into our Christian maturity, or lack thereof, as well. We desire to become spiritually mature, but we want that maturity to come by reading a daily devotional, or by simply attending a church service or Bible study on a weekly basis. We choose to not put in the hours and weeks and months and years of personal study, personal meditation, personal memorization, and personal application that is required to achieve any level of spiritual maturity.

The point is, there are no shortcuts. Our love of pleasure, our get-rich-quick attitude, our sprinter's mentality short-circuits any possibility of obtaining anything we truly desire. If you want to become financially successful, living like you already are wealthy and taking the shortcuts will not get you there. If you want to lose weight and enjoy good health, eating a salad once a week and doing ten sit-ups won't get you there. If you want to become spiritually mature, pretending you already are and snacking on spiritual food won't get you there.

Sprinting never got me anywhere—whether it was on the track or in my life. Slow down. Take the long, tried, and true method to success and maturity. It will have a positive effect on every area of your life.

* * *

TAKE ACTION

Take stock of all the distractions you allow in your daily routines, such as notification noises on your phone and computer. Start eliminating these distractions, or at least managing them to look at once or twice a day. Then begin to develop the art of focus, of giving your complete attention to what is important, not just what is clamoring for your attention.

CHAPTER 7

Danger Afoot

There was a television show that was popular in the 1960s called *Lost in Space*. It was a cheesy science fiction depiction of the Robinson family on a spaceship that got lost in the vast expanse of space and hopped from planet to planet in the attempt to find the earth. The young boy in the family was named Will. A robot followed Will around and would start flashing and beeping and thrashing his "arms" whenever danger was near, exclaiming, "*Danger, danger, Will Robinson!*"

Solomon isn't a robot, and you and I are not lost in space, but we often are lost in our approach to handling our finances. Traps and trickery and deception and falsehood fill the landscape of our financial world. For us to navigate properly and avoid these landmines, we need some help— some wisdom to recognize the signals and subtle ploys; the scams and insidious allurements; the seemingly harmless, accepted practices of our culture; and the deceitfulness of our own hearts.

God desperately wants us to avoid being hurt regarding the finances He so richly supplies. He has neither hidden His principles, nor has He made it difficult. God has revealed in plain and simple words what to be cautious with and what to comprehensively avoid. But He leaves it then for us to believe and apply, or to disbelieve and ignore.

We will dig in and discover some of what Solomon has to teach us on the topics of debt, overspending, and wastefulness in this chapter. The challenge is being raw and honest in our self-assessment, for most of us think we can handle coloring outside the lines in these vital areas.

The Value of Patience

The church I pastor is a small mountain congregation. From the opening of our church, I have always taken my turn leading the worship we do in song. We don't have a worship band or even an accomplished pianist, so we sing along with recorded music off CDs and digital files. In preparation for December one year, I ordered some Christmas CDs. I had found some great bargains on the Internet—I couldn't believe the prices. When they arrived, they sat on my desk for several weeks. When I finally listened to the CDs to pick out a few selections for the upcoming service, I discovered why they were so cheap. I couldn't possibly use them—I'm not sure how the company even allowed them to be recorded (I guess because they knew there would be people like me who would buy them).

The old adage "You get what you pay for" comes to mind; I invested only a little money and got the poor quality I should have expected. Closely related to this old adage is the biblical principle of sowing and reaping. This is the principle at work in the first three Proverbs we will glean from in this chapter. On the surface, they all seem to deal with how your actions affect your own life—but we must understand that what affects our life also affects those around us.

The first Proverb contrasts kindness and cruelty—"**The merciful man does himself good, but the cruel man does himself harm**" (11:17). Our sinful nature is selfish. It always has a strong tendency to "Look out for #1" in any given situation. I have often asked the question in sermons and Bible studies, "What is the opposite of love?" Inevitably, the first answer I get is "Hate." But I propose to you that the opposite of love is selfishness. True biblical love is always doing what is best for the other person—which is sometimes not what is best for yourself (selfishness). Those who choose cruelty over kindness may think they are looking out for themselves, but they are actually destroying themselves—and everyone around them. Be kind to those around you and you are actually being kind to yourself.

The point of our second Proverb deals with delayed gratification—**"The wicked earns deceptive wages, but he who sows righteousness gets a true reward"** (11:18). I remember a baseball player who, in his free agency, was able to sign a contract with the highest bidder. Many teams were offering him a lengthy contract worth millions each year, but one team offered him less up front and delayed a good portion of his contract over many additional years, with interest. He delayed the big up-front money and took the latter. This team ended up paying this player millions of dollars annually for seven years after this player had retired.

More so than our baseball player, if you live a godly life, your reward is eternal, not just for a few years into your retirement. Those who live their life without God are having their reward for the short time they live. One pastor said, *"The only heaven unbelievers experience is their life on this earth, and the only hell believers experience is their life on this earth."* Life on this earth is only temporary—live for the truly lasting rewards instead of the temporary pleasures of this world.

And the bottom line is summed up in the last Proverb of this triplet—**"He who is steadfast in righteousness will attain to life, and he who pursues evil will bring about his own death"** (11:19). The ultimate point of all the Proverbs Solomon wrote is the choice between eternal life and eternal death. Those who are godly will tend to make decisions that lead to eternal life while those who are evil will tend to make decisions that lead to eternal death.

Embracing and developing patience will serve you well in all aspects of life, and it is invaluable in your finances, but you must be prepared to battle against certain attitudes we tend to cultivate.

There is a warrior mentality that has been prevalent in our culture. The salesmen and saleswomen who travel, and those who earn their living as consultants are even labeled as "Road Warriors." A hotel chain has picked up on this perception to give those who travel a reason to take advantage of their accommodations—in essence, saying, "We understand the ravages of the daily grind." There is likely a measure of pride that comes along with being a road warrior.

In general, being a warrior is something you can hold your head up for; something you can be admired for. It brings to mind the Vikings of old and the men of yore who had to fight hand-to-hand to secure their homes and to capture tonight's dinner. Warriors are strong and resourceful, and the spoils of war are theirs for the taking.

Being known as a warrior, whether you are male or female, is a good thing. After all, the Scripture uses the analogy of us being in a spiritual battle every day of our Christian life. We are even given a list of the weapons of our warfare in Ephesians 6:10–20, and we are given some details about this battle in 2 Corinthians 10:3–5. "*Warrior good*," says Og. But there is another side to this coin.

Solomon wants us to examine another way that may be more suitable for the situations we find ourselves in on a daily basis—"**He who is slow to anger is better than the mighty, and he who rules over his spirit, than he who captures a city**" (16:32). If not held in check, having the warrior mentality can lead to impatience and a lack of self-control. And once you cross that line in one area of your life, you will easily cross that line in other areas.

Let me give you an example of how these disciplines feed off each other for good or bad. I have been overweight since my mid-thirties. Recently, I finally found the correct motivation to get healthier. In the past, my motivation was always in the realm of looking better—in other words, vanity. It wasn't until I recognized the benefit of improving my energy and mental focus for the various ministries God has graciously allowed me to be involved in that I was able to truly engage in healthier habits—and it has already made a huge impact.

The discipline and self-control required to pass by the bakery section of the grocery store without picking up a chocolate donut and a bear claw, and the discipline of going to the rec center to workout regularly, has spilled over into other areas of my life. Areas such as spending more time in prayer and the study of God's Word for the pleasure and benefit of knowing God more intimately, instead of just studying to prepare a Bible study or sermon. This discipline also spilled over into finally writing this book. I also now have a "can-do" attitude about many other things.

Conversely, when I cave in to the temptation and lose self-control in one area of my life, it makes it easier to falter in other areas of my life; I become lazy and apathetic in much more than just that initial lapse.

I have recognized the warrior mentality asserting itself as these disciplines are cultivated and built up, but I have also noticed that a great amount of patience is required for the desired results to be manifest. God says, **"He who is slow to anger is better than the mighty, and he who rules over his spirit, than he who captures a city."**

So, when you are out there today making your next conquest, whether it is closing a sale, traveling, or teaching a three-year-old to tie his shoes, be a patient warrior. We are warriors in the spiritual sense at all times, and most times we must be warriors in the physical and emotional sense, but we must employ patience and have self-control in the various battles we face.

What a Waste!

As a high school senior approaching graduation, I had no clue what I wanted to do with my life, nor did I have any inkling of whether I should attend college or which one. A representative from DeVry Institute of Technology set an appointment and came to my home to meet with me and my parents. They were the only school who did this. Since no one else apparently wanted me, I applied for some student loans, applied for entrance into the school, and, the following fall, I started attending classes.

It wasn't long before I realized that I had no interest in electronics engineering. DeVry is a technical school with very few choices as to specializing your education, as opposed to a college where you have all kinds of choices. But since I had already made my decision, I stuck with it for four trimesters—accumulating a growing amount of debt on my student loan. During the summer trimester, it became exceedingly difficult for me to give my classes the amount of time required for understanding the material. (It also didn't help that Wrigley Field was only a few miles away with Cub games starting at 1:20 p.m. and my classes starting at 2:00 p.m.) My heart simply was not in this area of knowledge I was half-heartedly pursuing. I was only wasting money (on school and on the many Cub games I attended).

Solomon deals with this heart attitude in today's Proverb—"**Why is there a price in the hand of a fool to buy wisdom, when he has no sense?**" (17:16)

While I was not opposed to all knowledge and wisdom, I was opposed to learning about electronics engineering. I was essentially a fool because of how I squandered my money on something I had no interest in. True fools, in the biblical sense, are those who do not seek any wisdom or knowledge, especially the knowledge and wisdom of God. Solomon is not reprimanding the fools but is warning those who would throw money away by attempting to force the fool to learn. It can't be done! It is senseless!

So, as teachers of God's Word and His principles (and all of us are teachers in one sense or another), we must be careful to devote our time to those who have a hunger and a thirst for God's wisdom. When we try to force this education on those who do not have the heart for it, we are throwing our time and our money away. In Matthew 10:14, Jesus says to His disciples, "**Whoever does not receive you, nor heed your words, as you go out of that house or city, shake the dust off your feet.**" Do not waste your time trying to teach God's principles to those who do not want it.

This does not mean that we do not witness to the lost, but it does mean that we are to be good stewards of our time by focusing on those who show an interest, as opposed to those who shut us down all the time. Pray that God will stir an interest in his or her heart and then move on. The same goes for Christians who have no interest in Bible studies; don't force them or guilt trip them into attending. Pray that God would stir their heart to desire to attend, and then move on.

And, at the risk of possibly offending you since you have invested your money into this book, and thus have shown an interest in improving your understanding of handling money as God desires – do something with any knowledge and wisdom you pick up from Solomon's words. Otherwise, you may find yourself in the place of this next character Solomon describes.

"I passed by the field of the sluggard and by the vineyard of the man lacking sense, and behold, it was completely overgrown with thistles; its surface was covered with nettles, and its stone wall was broken down. When I saw, I reflected upon it; I looked, and received instruction. 'A little sleep, a little slumber, a little folding of the hands to rest,' then your poverty will come as a robber and your want like an armed man" (24:30–34).

"What a waste!" We all have made this statement when we see something that shouldn't be. Maybe you see a fine piece of artwork that has been damaged due to negligence or carelessness; a nice car or truck needs a new engine because the owner never changed or even checked their oil; maybe it's a house that has been neglected and in need of major repairs when a little regular maintenance would have done the trick previously; or worst of all, maybe you see a person's life going down the tubes due to laziness. It's sad to see *things* wasted, but it is a tragedy to see a *life* wasted.

The person Solomon uses in his Proverb is lazy. And let me describe laziness before you start imagining all of the people you know who need to read this. Laziness comes in many forms. You may be a dynamo on the job, or quick to volunteer your services when called upon, and still be lazy in the greater sense of the word. Procrastination is laziness. Putting off doing what is necessary because it is not pleasant is laziness. I have known people who lost their job and have the ability to draw unemployment but don't, because they will not go through the hassle of filing the paperwork. I have known others who had a good paying job but quit because they didn't like the work, even though they had no other immediate prospects for employment.

Let me share a few other examples of laziness that most likely affect all of us at times.

- You watch four hours of television at night but only fifteen minutes (if that) reading your Bible.
- You say you need to get in better shape, but another day goes by without any physical exercise.
- Your financial life is a mess, but you never take the time to consult God's Word on the topic (this obviously does not apply to you).

Laziness, in sum, is simply not doing what is necessary at the time that it needs to be done. Laziness is surrendering in the daily battle with your propensity to waste your time on the trivial.

I could go on, but this is getting a little too uncomfortable (for me!). The point is we procrastinate in so many areas of our lives, and procrastination is just a fancier word for laziness, and laziness leads to poverty—poverty of mind, poverty of spirit, poverty of understanding and wisdom, poverty of good health, and, obviously, poverty in the financial sense.

And make sure you do not miss the fact that poverty is a guaranteed outcome of laziness according to this Proverb, not just a possible outcome. What a waste indeed! But there's more.

In the early years of my marriage, I made the comment to my wife that we should not have any plastic containers in the house. My reasoning was that we had a great tendency to put our leftovers in these containers, stick them in the back of the fridge, and then, two months later, throw away what used to be food, and have to then scrub and sanitize the containers so it could be used for our next science experiment. During that phase of our lives, we rarely ate leftovers, but, deep within us, we found it hard to throw perfectly good food away, so it went in the containers. It was okay to throw it away after it turned green and fuzzy, but it went against the grain to throw it away prior to that.

I have grown to appreciate these containers as I scrubbed and sanitized my attitude and mindset on the value of money. God opened my eyes to how wasteful I had been and now it is much more likely we will eat all of the leftovers before they spoil. I eat the crumbs at the bottom of the potato chip bag, I turn bottles of lotion upside down—sometimes even cutting the bottle open to get every last smear of lotion—I roll and squeeze and roll and squeeze the toothpaste container to make sure none goes to waste, etc.

Most of us struggle with wasting something of value, especially if you grew up in a home where the previous generations either experienced the Great Depression or had been told about it so often; it is forever etched in their brains. The generation of the Baby Boomers and ever since, though, have progressively become less concerned about wasting things. Virtually everything is temporary and disposable.

"A man who loves wisdom makes his father glad, but he who keeps company with harlots wastes his wealth" (29:3).

Solomon gives us an obvious example of waste, but the principle goes far beyond spending money for sex. The general principle is that it is wise to conserve and foolish to waste. In our American culture, we really do not understand the meaning of true wisdom in this regard. We are somewhat clueless at the staggering amount of money we waste over our lifetimes.

A $2,000/month mortgage payment typically has $1,800–$1,900 of interest included, especially in the early years of the mortgage. The interest on credit cards is designed to keep you in debt once you get into the habit of carrying a balance. If you have a $1,000 balance and only pay the minimum payment without charging anything else, it will take twelve to fifteen years to pay it off, and the interest you pay will end up being more than the $1,000 you charged. We purchase brand new cars that lose up to 20% of their value the moment you drive it off the lot. A prominent financial teacher, author, and radio host calls things of this nature a "Stupid Tax."

The primary issue, other than having a lack of wisdom, is we are not content. We want new stuff and we want it now. Waiting on the Lord is not a concept we want anything to do with. Being content in your circumstances is obsolete. And, by the way, when we lack contentment and we are dissatisfied with anything, you are essentially saying you are dissatisfied with God—so be careful.

Take an inventory of your life. Find areas where you are wasteful and start making the necessary changes. There is great wisdom in conserving what you have. I guess having some plastic containers around is not so bad after all.

The Insidious Nature of Debt

I commend you for hanging in there with me. We hate talking about debt. We have been conditioned by our culture that debt is the normal way of life; everyone has a car payment, mortgage, and a generous stash of credit cards. You simply can't get by in our culture without debt, right? Again, since you are still with me, I commend you; you are taking the first step to financial freedom in the simple affirmation that debt, as a way of life, is a myth, and a destructive myth at that. So, let's add to what I started at the end of that last Proverb.

There was a time in my life as a young husband and father when I was clueless and full of pride (well, maybe more than just a single time in my life). This particular time, we were in debt way over our heads, the job situation was not all that it had been just a year or two earlier, and it was getting hard to figure out a way through the mess.

One evening during this time, the associate pastor from our church showed up at our doorstep with several bags of groceries. I plastered a feigned smile on my face and thanked him for the kindness but inside I was furious and embarrassed. How did he know that we were in such bad shape, and, if he knew, how many others knew?

I was more so mad at myself because I was clueless in how to handle money. I was of the mindset that, if I could handle the minimum monthly payments, I was okay. Debt wasn't a concern to me. Buy now, pay later were some of the sweetest words I knew. And yet, somehow in the midst of this ignorance I was wallowing in, I thought I had it all together. So, to be smacked in the face with the reality that other people had to make sure we had food on the table ...

"A man's pride will bring him low, but a humble spirit will obtain honor" (29:23).

If you believe you have your life together, the principles contained in this nugget of wisdom could act as a timely reminder, but be careful; often, those who think they have it all together are indeed thinking from a position of pride. And this is the real issue—those who need to learn from this Proverb typically do not think they have a problem. I didn't think I had a problem, and, unfortunately, my pride brought me low time and time again until I finally began to learn the lessons. So, take a moment to ponder these principles even if you believe you have it all together.

I won't go so far as to say I now have a humble spirit. (Can you ever really say that and not be doing so from a position of pride?) But I can say I have finally learned the dangers of debt. My wife and I are working toward being completely debt-free. The land and church building my congregation acquired was also debt-free by the miraculous hand of God, but it took having my pride crushed several times to reach this point of understanding.

I have used an example from my life concerning handling personal finances, but the issue of pride is much more pervasive than just this one area. What's yours? Do you have an unhealthy pride in your education? How about your level of spiritual maturity? It is common to come across Christians who believe they have achieved a higher plane in their spiritual life, and thus look down upon us peasants who don't quite get it. Maybe you struggle with pride because of your elevated position at work, at church, in the community, or even your social status. Or maybe you, too, have trouble admitting you are clueless, or next to clueless, at handling money.

Whatever your area of weakness may be, understand that Solomon is not telling you that your pride *might* bring you low but that it will. Better to take heed now and correct the problem than to have this Proverb come to fruition in your life and cause you to experience being furious and embarrassed like I was.

When we refuse to humble ourselves, especially with our cluelessness about handling our finances, we can drag others into our mess and cause them pain.

It seems like it is a rite of passage—at least in today's American culture. Each generation becomes more callous or uncaring about it. What once was embarrassing to even consider is now like any other phone call or conversation. I'm talking about living beyond our means and relying on the sympathy and generosity of your parents to make ends meet.

I've "been there done that" on more than one occasion during my earlier years of adulthood. If I am not mistaken, my parents even cash advanced credit cards at times to help me out the self-inflicted financial jams I got in. The first time I felt the need to ask for help was excruciating. The second time, it was embarrassing. The times after that were uncomfortable but it was becoming old hat as I reached the point of presuming upon or expecting the help to always be there.

This is the thrust of this next Proverb—**"He who robs his father or his mother and says, 'It is not a transgression,' is the companion of a man who destroys"** (28:24).

Now, obviously, if you literally steal from your parents, that is wrong on many levels, but the underlying issue is more along the lines of taking advantage of them to bail you out of your financial foolishness of not living within your means. My parents always did what they could to help and they never showed any disdain or disappointment in me for not handling my finances properly. Living within your means is a life of not having to borrow, use credit cards, and staying current on your other bills and purchases; and, I will add, having funds left over to give and to save or invest.

This is a foreign concept in our culture today. The term "cash is king" has been replaced by "credit is king." Just watch the television commercials or listen to the radio ads. You can't watch or listen for more than thirty minutes without seeing or hearing multiple spots dealing with your credit score or how to reduce your monthly payments, etc. Most "experts" say, to have a great credit score, you have to have multiple loans and carry balances on your credit cards; the loans must have a perfect payment history and the cards can't have high balances or late payments; but, nonetheless, to have a great credit score, you must have a measure of debt. The Bible is clear that debt as a way of life is wrong and always dangerous.

The paradigm shift, each generation has experienced regarding credit and debt (at least, since the Great Depression) is what leads many to violate the principles of our Proverb. Whether a person literally steals from their parents or presumes upon their generosity, it is indeed a transgression and puts you in bad company.

One other aspect of this principle is made clear for us by Jesus in Matthew 15:4–9, where He blasts the pharisees for withholding help to their parents because they had supposedly given all their money to the Temple treasury. I doubt any of them had given all their money to the Temple treasury; it was most likely just an excuse to get out of providing for their elderly parents. Regardless of how their financial situation was, Jesus made it clear that they had an obligation to provide for their parents during their time of need. And I submit to you that withholding that help is also a form of stealing from your parents.

Whether or not you have had to seek help from your parents, or they are in a position where they need help, the point of it all is to make sure you are following the many principles God has left us in His Word for handling money and possessions. If we all did this, there would not be a need to consider what this Proverb is teaching us.

This next Proverb is, in my opinion, the pinnacle of wisdom on the topic of debt.

"The rich rules over the poor, and the borrower becomes the lender's slave" (22:7).

I have been, and still am, a slave. I admit I know nothing of slavery in the terms most Americans think of from the inception and early years of our country, but, in the biblical sense, I am a slave. This is both a good and a bad condition to be in—depending upon whom your master is.

The Apostle Paul, among many others, referred to himself as the slave, servant, bondservant, etc., of Jesus Christ on many occasions throughout the Scripture. In Bible times and in many cases, slavery was a desired occupation. Slavery, or indentured servitude, was more like contract work in today's society. A person would sign on to work for a master as a "keeper of the household or property" for a set number of years (usually seven) for a specified salary. This person and his family would live on the property and receive food and shelter along with their salary. At the end of seven years, they were free to go, or they could choose by mutual agreement to sign on for life. If this happened, in most cultures, the "slave" would then have his ear pierced and an earring would be attached to represent that he belonged to his master for life. All in all, many of the "slaves" of these times lived a much better quality of life than the average person.

There is obviously also a negative side of slavery. Some of the slavery in Bible times comes closer to our normal understanding of the term—forced slavery, brutal conditions, and horrible treatment with no way out.

I have lived this Proverb on more than one occasion. The debts I owe have indeed put me in a position of being the slave to my lenders. My choices in life are, many times, governed by if I can afford it.

Not too many years ago, my desire and calling to be a pastor on a full-time basis was controlled by my lenders. They said I could not afford to give up my insurance business and my wife could not afford to be a full-time wife and ministry partner. If I did not have debt, the choices would have been different at that time in my life. In this way, I was a slave to my lenders because I was not free to make other choices.

Solomon opens our eyes to the stark reality of using credit. This would resonate even more with his original audience. In those times there were no rules and laws (outside of God's Law to Israel) regarding loans. A lender could charge whatever fees and interest he wanted and set whatever terms he wanted. Taking out a loan in those times more resembled today's loan sharks than today's banks. We don't have "debtor's prisons" anymore ... or do we?

Work on eliminating your debts. Stop using credit cards, especially if you cannot pay them off completely when the monthly bill comes. Let's work on being a slave to Christ alone, and not a slave to banks and other lending institutions. Imagine the possibilities if the people of the church were totally free to serve Jesus wholly and undividedly, and if they had all that money that is going to interest payments for ministry instead.

So, what does Solomon have to say concerning loans of any type?

Borrowing and Cosigning

"Buy now, pay later" really means, "Buy now, pay later, then pay some more later, and then pay even more later." Although the invention of the credit card is from our fairly recent history, the concept of "buy now, pay later" has been around for as long as the desire to have things has been around.

Solomon warns us to be very cautious in regards to allowing someone else to "buy now, pay later" when you are the one who may have to take care of the "pay" part—**My son, if you have become surety for your neighbor, have given a pledge for a stranger, if you have been snared with the words of your mouth, have been caught with the words of your mouth ... "** (6:1-2a). Before we go too far, let's understand the culture in which this was written. Then we can better understand how to apply this wisdom to our own lives.

Those who preyed upon the weak (meaning the ones who had a penchant for spending money they did not have on things they did not need) always did so with an eye toward their companions. They knew the spendthrift had no viable means of paying the debt they were about to incur, but, if they could find the right companion who would cosign, they could take him for all he was worth. It was really an ancient ancestor to our modern day "Loan Sharks." It was not uncommon to expect five to ten times the amount of the loan in return. And these loans were sometimes due on demand—they didn't have a six-months same as cash option. They could demand payment at pretty much any time with all of the interest due with it. If a friend cosigned, the laws of the land said they were responsible for the debt, not the one who purchased the goods. In those days, delinquent debtors went to prison until the debt was paid.

Is it any wonder that Solomon tells us, if you find yourself in the position of being surety on a loan (a cosigner), he then said, **"do this then, my son, and deliver yourself; since you have come into the hand of your neighbor, go, humble yourself, and importune your neighbor. Give no sleep to your eyes, nor slumber to your eyelids; deliver yourself like a gazelle from the hunter's hand and like a bird from the hand of the fowler"** (6:2b–5; also see 11:15, 17:18, and 22:26–27).

By cosigning a loan, you are like a trapped animal. When an animal gets in a trap, does he sit there and ponder his predicament? No, he struggles and fights and kicks and claws to get out of the trap. This is how Solomon tells us to react when faced with being the guarantee on someone else's loan. You are the one who is trapped, not the other person.

So, how do we apply this today?

Is this passage a proof text for those who refuse to ever lend money? First, we must remember the overall point of the Book of Proverbs—to pursue wisdom and understanding. Secondly, we must know what the rest of the Scripture has to say on the subject of loans and surety; we are pursuing wisdom and understanding from God's Word in handling loans and surety.

Let's quickly and briefly look at some general principles from the Bible concerning borrowing money:

- If you borrow you must repay. Psalm 37:21 calls you wicked if you do not repay. Borrowing money is almost invariably a simple lack of patience, of wanting something before you have saved the money to have it. Because of this impatience and/or lack of contentment, we waste God's provision on unnecessary interest payments.

Because of buildings and other purchases, many major denominations pay out more in interest every year than they do on ministry, as do many individual churches. I am sure that many Christians also pay more in interest payments than they put in the offering plate.

- Borrowing presumes upon God if you do not have the liquid means to repay now. James 4:13–17 gives us this principle of presuming upon the future, or presuming upon God's provision. When we borrow based only upon the future ability to pay, we are presuming upon God's goodness in giving us the means to earn that money in the future. We don't know what tomorrow holds. If the loan is not based upon our current means to pay in full, we are presuming upon God's goodness and provision.
- Understand the immense risk you take and the severe limitations you accept on your life, when you borrow. We already considered Proverbs 22:7 but Deuteronomy 28:43–45 teaches us the same principle that we become slave to the lender when we borrow. In many ways, we belong to them when we owe.

Many Christians have sensed the call of God on their life to go into full-time ministry, whether it is on the mission field, or to pastor a church, or to start a ministry of some sort. But they are so far in debt, with no immediate means to get out, that they cannot leave their current jobs to follow God. They are in bondage to their lenders.

So, I trust we understand the serious nature of borrowing money along with giving us the motivation to extract ourselves from that bondage. There are several wonderful programs available that can help you, from a biblical perspective, to take the necessary steps toward being debt-free. You need to plug into one of these programs, but I'll give you the first few commonly accepted steps in most any program:

1. STOP borrowing, which for most of us that means to stop adding to your debt by using credit cards.

2. Accumulate a modest emergency fund of $500–$1,000 in a simple savings account. This is important because it gives a little room to handle the inevitable emergencies of life without falling back on using a credit card.

3. Use the snowball method of eliminating your debts. Start with the lowest balance, regardless of the interest rate. Pay as much as possible on that balance each month while doing minimum payments on the others. Once that smallest balance is paid off completely, snowball or add whatever you have been paying on that smallest balance to the next smallest balance along with the minimum you were paying. Then just keep rolling those amounts onto the next.

My wife and I have used this snowball method, and it works like a charm. God enabled us to eliminate over $35,000 of debt in about three years.

So, what about lending money to others? The Bible is all over this one.

Psalm 37:26 – **"All day long he is gracious and lends, and his descendants are a blessing."**

Psalm 112:5 – **"It is well with the man who is gracious and lends; he will maintain his cause in judgment."**

Matthew 5:42 – **"Give to him who asks of you, and do not turn away from him who wants to borrow from you."**

Luke 6:34-36 – **"If you lend to those from whom you expect to receive, what credit is that to you? Even sinners lend to sinners in order to receive back the same amount. But love your enemies, and do good, and lend, expecting nothing in return; and your reward will be great, and you will be sons of the Most High; for He Himself is kind to ungrateful and evil men. Be merciful, just as your Father is merciful."**

According to God, we are to do all we can to avoid borrowing money, but we are to freely and generously lend money, even if there isn't much hope of ever seeing that money again. I think most of us have the equation backwards. We are quick to borrow (and remember, using credit cards are a form of borrowing) but we are very cautious and even miserly about lending. And, if you really want to see God's heart and His intent in the practice of lending money, read Exodus 22:25, Deuteronomy 23:19–20, and Psalm 15:5 for starters. In these and other passages, you will discover that God does not allow you to charge interest on your personal loans to others.

We have another Proverb that teaches us that we must, sometimes, step in with drastic measures to rescue others from making poor decisions with borrowing money.

"Take his garment when he becomes surety for a stranger; and for foreigners, hold him in pledge" (20:16).

This is a fascinating principle. There are times when you have to step into a situation to stop someone from making a horrible mistake. Some people just do not have the practical wisdom to avoid the dangers and pitfalls of life. All throughout the Book of Proverbs, we have admonitions for foolish actions and foolish people. They either do not know any better or they don't care. This Proverb deals with those who don't know any better and it is the responsibility of the wise to step in and help them make the right decisions.

The principle involved in this Proverb lies in the fact that fools are prone to enter into shady financial deals. It looks good to them on the outside, but they are unaware of the dangers that lurk in the shadows.

The implication for all of this is twofold. First, don't play the fool when it comes to "your" finances. I have quotations around the word "your" because they really aren't yours. God gives us the power to make wealth, and it is He who provides the health and ability to earn a living, and it is He who opens the opportunities for the jobs we have and have had. Don't fall for get-rich-quick schemes, don't make risky investment decisions, and don't get involved with shady business deals.

Secondly, we who have learned the financial principles outlined for us in the Bible need to be aware of those around us who are about to make bad choices when it comes to the use of God's money. This Proverb would better be understood as taking the collateral away from the person who is about to use it unwisely. In other words, do what you have to do to essentially sabotage the opportunity. Don't look at it as intruding into someone's personal business, look at it as helping preserve God's money.

And since we are told to love one another repeatedly in the Scripture, just how loving is it to knowingly allow a brother or sister in Christ to make a foolish decision in this regard?

Spending Wisely

How much is enough? Can you quantify enough? Can you place a number on enough? Is there such a thing as enough in the lives of most people—or do we always want more?

One of the great wealth barons of the early 1900s was once interviewed by a newspaper reporter. The reporter asked the question, "How much money will be enough for you?" The man answered along the lines of, "More than I have today." His attitude is the same as most Americans today. Most of us always want more than we currently have—no matter what level of wealth and possessions we find ourselves at.

Solomon is once again speaking to us about contentment and the contrast between godly gain and wicked gain—"**Great wealth is in the house of the righteous, but trouble is in the income of the wicked**" (15:6). God is giving us a promise—if we live a godly, righteous life, we will always not only have enough, but we will have a surplus. We will have the necessities of life in storage in our households. On the other side of the equation, He is promising that the gain of the wicked will bring them only trouble.

This Proverb is not promising great wealth to the godly or even promising that the godly will always be in the upper middle classes of society, it is simply stating that the godly will always have enough. Which brings us back to the question, "How much is enough?"

Most Americans have a skewed sense of what the necessities of life are. If you took an American family that is in debt and barely able to keep food on the table, and you stole their television, inside of a week or so, they will find a way to get a new television. They can't pay their bills, but they will get a new television.

The godly will always be provided for in the necessities of life. The psalmist says in Psalm 37:25, "**I have been young and now I am old, yet I have not seen the righteous forsaken or his descendants begging bread.**"

I fear that far too many Christians are looking for material blessing in this world, and somehow thinking that it is their God-given right. We claim verses like Psalm 37:4, which says, "**Delight yourself in the Lord; and He will give you the desires of your heart,**" while not taking seriously and investing themselves in the first half of the verse; the desires of your heart will most definitely NOT be on financial and material blessing if you are truly delighting yourself in the Lord and are wholly focused on Him.

We also do not account for, "**The heart is more deceitful than all else and is desperately sick; Who can understand it?**" (Jeremiah 17:9) We cannot trust our hearts, and thus we cannot know exactly what our heart's desire is. In our mind's eye our heart's desire is most likely not what is best for us.

It may seem that I am straying way off topic here but bear with me just a little longer. The **wealth**, or the *abundant storage* as the Hebrew word has the sense of, that we are promised from God is based upon our physical needs, not our desires. All throughout the Scripture, God tries time and again to teach us contentment with what we have and where we are in life's journey—in other words, contentment in Him. When it comes to our material well-being, contentment is the key. It is our lack of contentment that causes us to buy more house than we need, or nicer cars than we need, or more "stuff" than we need. The Apostle Paul, in his first letter to Timothy, affirms that contentment is the key—he even says, "**But godliness actually is a means of great gain when accompanied by contentment**" (1 Timothy 6:6), and he emphasizes contentment as being the key a few verses later when he warns, "**But those who want to get rich fall into temptation and a snare and many foolish and harmful desires which plunge men into ruin and destruction. For the love of money is a root of all sorts of evil, and some by longing for it have wandered away from the faith and pierced themselves with many griefs**" (6:9–10). And, do not allow your heart to deceive you at this moment by believing that you are the exception and could handle great wealth.

Overspending is what puts most of us in the hole, which creates a domino effect of so many other issues in our life. We spend more than we should and, when the tough times come (and they will come), we have a crisis of faith wondering why God isn't sending us a check. If we focus too long on our circumstances and begin to have our own little pity party, we begin to question God and His Word (usually because we have misinterpreted His Word). Let this go on too long and you now have a wandering Christian who is blaming God for his problems. If you trace it back, what is he blaming God for? He is blaming God for the fact the he or she overspent—not being content. If we are not careful, we will place ourselves on the wrong side of this Proverb—the side where **trouble is in the income of the wicked.**

Learn contentment. Learn to pray as Jesus taught His disciples, "**Give us this day our daily bread**" (Matthew 6:11), not give us this day enough bread for the year. You will then be on the path of living a godly and righteous life, which will then lead to having *abundant storage.*

There is another Proverb on this issue of overspending. This one deals with spending everything you get.

My dad used to have a little comment regarding my mom's love of finding bargains while shopping, "*Your mother has saved me so much money, I should be rich!*" The problem was, my mom would buy things whether she had any immediate need or use in mind if it was a good enough deal. Their closets and cabinets were full of bargains and deals she found over the years. Now, granted, she was never at a loss when an unexpected party, wedding shower, or baby shower came around, but I believe even she admitted she had gone a little overboard.

I am not calling my mom a fool by using her as an example today, for she was a very frugal shopper and she was abundantly generous with everything she had, but I did want to use our appetite for shopping to illustrate this last Proverb for this chapter—**"There is precious treasure and oil in the dwelling of the wise, but a foolish man swallows it up"** (21:20).

Your ability to be content, will be the primary factor in determining if you will have enough later in life. One of the most admirable qualities of the wise is this contentedness we have been observing. They do not have all the latest and greatest toys and gadgets and feel no compulsion to accumulate such. They buy frugally as they have need, and they buy quality because they know, in the long run, high quality is less expensive than cheap. They do not get suckered into buying items just because the advertising was enticing, or their friend bought one.

The following is, apparently, a parable or illustration that someone created, as I have never been able to confirm any validity of this being a factual account. But it does an excellent job of making an important point.

A company constructed a factory in a remote area of another less developed country. The local people lived very simply, many in mud and straw homes, but the company had no problem recruiting enough workers to run the plant. After the first two weeks, everything was running very smoothly. The local people were hard working and got along with each other very well. At the end of the second week, the first batch of paychecks was handed out. The next Monday, more than half of the workforce did not show up. The meager paychecks, by most standards, were more money than most of them needed for the year. When you are used to living off the land, what are you going to do with money?

The company had a big problem. How do you motivate people to come back to work when they do not need money? One executive in the company came up with the idea of sending catalogs from the major retailers to the homes of all the workers. Within a few short weeks, just about everybody returned to the factory. They now had "stuff" to spend money on and the paycheck was now "required" for them to live.

Every time I hear or use that story, it is a sobering reminder to me of how much money I spend simply because I am discontent with what I have. I play the fool when I spend all the money I earn (and then some when I use credit to make the purchase).

I hear people often say, *"If I had a lot of money."* They prove they are not ready for wealth by spouting off all the things they would buy. Do not miss the implication of Solomon's words. Contentedness is the path to true wealth. Why? Because being content will have a drastic effect on what you spend today and what you need to live comfortably in the future.

By all means, learn the principles of handling money, and then earn everything God enables you to earn. But then spend wisely and be content with what God blesses you with.

* * *

TAKE ACTION

Swallow your pride and accept the fact that you do not know it all when it comes to handling your finances. I will even suggest that you accept the fact that you don't even know what is best for you when it comes to handling your finances. Now, approach each financial decision with great care and caution. Make today the day that you stop being so casual with money.

CHAPTER 8

SETTING YOURSELF UP FOR DISAPPOINTMENT

As an eight-year-old, I was already becoming the "big man on campus." I was the kid everyone wanted to be around. That summer, an accident to my right eye almost blinded me in that eye and caused my left eye to quickly become nearsighted. I was too young to get acclimated to or be bothered by the daily regimen of contact lenses, so I began wearing eyeglasses to begin the following school year. This was in the late 1960s, and eyeglasses were not cool. My popularity plummeted.

This was a blessing in disguise in many ways, but probably the greatest benefit of essentially dropping out of the social scene was discovering our local library. My love for reading was spawned that year. I would visit the library sometimes multiple times each week, check out a few books, climb a tree in our backyard, and read for hours at a time.

This love for reading has served me well through the years (especially when God called me to be a pastor). In my late twenties and still today, I enjoy reading motivational and self-help books. For reasons unbeknownst to me, I struggle with negativity and the motivational materials helped stave off completely succumbing to this harmful attitude. But while the motivation helped with my attitude and outlook, I rarely followed through on the activities promoted in these books to bring more substantial positive change to my life. I would get excited at the prospect of making things better but would be disappointed instead from my lack of application.

Since you invested in this book, it is safe to assume that you desire to make at least a few changes in how you currently handle your finances. And I am confident that, if you take seriously what God has said through Solomon, and if you diligently apply these concepts, positive change will inevitably take place. But there are some cautionary tales we must consider.

So, in this chapter we will look at a few falsehoods from Solomon's wisdom. False expectations, false impressions, false security, misplaced trust, and the dangers of a dream mentality—dreams are important, but they must be based in truth.

False Expectations

I look for ways to cut corners as often as I can. For as long as I have been married, my wife is still dumbfounded at times when I bring the groceries in the house. I will have as many bags in my arms and wrapped around my fingers as is humanly possible, so I can make less trips back and forth. Occasionally, I end up dropping a bag or having to let it down harder and faster than I would like because my capacity to hang on any longer has reached its limit. And, of course, the bag I drop is the one with the eggs in it.

Have you ever considered laziness as being destructive? I'm not sure you can label my penchant for carrying more bags to make less trips as lazy or just stupid. I probably expend more energy carrying the heavier loads than I would have walking back and forth an extra time or two. Other examples would probably be better illustrations of the point, but Solomon wants us to understand that laziness is, indeed, destructive—**"He also who is slack in his work is brother to him who destroys"** (18:9).

A better illustration might be of a builder who doesn't take the time to properly construct a foundation for a house just to get the job done quicker and cheaper. When the house prematurely starts to fall apart, it is as bad as if someone came in and purposely started tearing it down. That being said, I want to make a spiritual application of this principle for us today. What are some ways that we can become spiritually lazy and how can that be destructive?

Let's take the spiritual discipline of reading and studying your Bible for an example. First, how is it that we can read and study our Bibles in a lazy manner? You could skip reading on the days when your schedule is a little overloaded. You could read it as if you took the "Evelyn Wood Speed Reading" course. You could half-heartedly listen to the Bible on tape or CD in the car or at home while your mind is on several other things. You could read your Bible when you are exhausted and lying in bed, drifting off for the night.

In our financial lives, we can be lazy by not taking the time to understand and employ even a simple budget. We can spend our money with no regard for next week or month, let alone next year and beyond. We can allow impulse purchases to be our primary method of shopping instead of having a plan. We can ignore calculating and then saving money for the inevitable "emergencies" of repairing and replacing appliances, vehicles, furnaces, roofs, etc., and instead go into debt when these inevitabilities occur.

So, how can habits like the ones mentioned above be destructive? Laziness in the intake of the Scripture will cause you to, at best, have a superficial knowledge of the Scripture and, at worst, have a totally wrong knowledge of the Scripture. This can be destructive to you by giving you unfounded hopes or unrealistic expectations. Laziness with your finances will destroy your peace, set you up for crippling debt, and deceive you in untold number of ways.

Let's say you quickly read Malachi 3:10, which says, "**Bring the whole tithe into the storehouse, so that there may be food in My house, and test Me now in this,' says the Lord of hosts, 'if I will not open for you the windows of heaven and pour out for you a blessing until it**

overflows.'" Without doing a full study of the context of this verse and seeing the rest of what God says concerning tithes and giving, you could easily believe that God is going to make you wealthy if you give your tithes to the church. When you do not become wealthy, you could stop giving altogether and possibly become disillusioned as to the reliability of the Bible.

Nowhere in the Scripture does God promise you wealth and riches in *this* life; there are some passages that imply material wealth if your life is completely devoted to God, but there is not an iron-clad guarantee of wealth. This verse from Malachi in particular isn't even directed at the church. We can gain a tremendous principle from it that can be applied in several ways to the church, but the promise in this verse is for Israel if they obeyed the Law of Moses in supporting the priesthood and "government" of the Jewish society. And, even if you could make the transition to us today and somehow think that the **"storehouse"** is representative of the church, **"blessing"** doesn't necessarily translate into material wealth. And your Christian life can be damaged or destroyed by a wrong and lazy interpretation of the Scripture.

The same can apply to the verses in the Bible that refer to our finances in other ways, many of which we have looked at in this book. If we are lazy in our studies, we can easily assume promises that are not there, and the false expectations we create in our mind can be damaging.

We must take the time and put in the hours of study before claiming a promise of the Scripture. Make sure you fully understand what the whole of Scripture says on a subject before you claim it for your life. Claiming something God is not really saying and expecting it to come to pass can very easily become destructive to you and to those around you. It could even destroy your faith and confidence in God's Word.

Don't be lazy and thus ensure that your expectations are based in truth.

False Security

"*Seeing is believing*"—so the saying goes. Our human nature can more easily relate to things we can touch and smell and taste—stuff we can hold onto. We generally long for security and we prefer to place our security in what our eyes can see and in what our hands can feel. Why? Why do we prefer the things we can see and hold? Because they give us the illusion of control, and make no mistake in your thinking, it is an illusion of control.

Solomon speaks to us today by showing us true and false security in these two Proverbs—**"The name of the Lord is a strong tower; the righteous runs into it and are safe. A rich man's wealth is his strong city, and like a high wall in his own imagination"** (18:10–11).

Let's take these in reverse order. False security is the security we place in the things we can see and touch (read Isaiah chapters 2 and 3 for some vivid illustrations of the folly of placing your security in "things"). Picture in your mind some physical things that bring you a sense of security. Maybe it's a large castle of stone, or a large sturdy house of log or brick. Maybe it's a hefty bank account and no debt. Maybe it's a loving and faithful spouse or parent. For some of you, it may even be a prominent position with a stable company or a thriving ministry. Whatever it may be, is there truly any legitimate security in these things?

Houses, and even stone castles, can be destroyed. Riches and wealth can disappear overnight as what happened during the Great Depression, or it can be stolen out from under you. Spouses and parents can drop dead right before your eyes, and jobs and positions of prominence are about as secure as grass hut in a hurricane. All of these things, and anything else you can imagine from a physical or material perspective, are illusions of security. They may provide some temporary security in your mind, but it is only in your mind, or imagination as our Proverb states. Just as your life is compared to a vapor in James 4:14, so too are the physical and material things we place our security in.

True security can only be found in one thing, and that is the Lord. The Lord is eternal. The Lord is infinite in power. There is no end to the Lord's love for you. There is no end to the Lord's care for you. Romans 8:38–39 says, **"For I am convinced that neither death, nor life, nor angels, nor principalities, nor things present, nor things to come, nor powers, nor height, nor depth, nor any other created thing, will be able to separate us from the love of God, which is in Christ Jesus."**

Now, that is the definition of security! Nothing, absolutely nothing, can separate us from God's love! That means even you can't do anything on your part to separate yourself from God's love. Once you have become a genuine Christian believer, there is no sin you can commit that will cause God to say, *"Okay, now you've done it. You went too far this time. I no longer love you."* It simply cannot happen!

We opened this section with a popular saying; let me end by reversing that saying. *"Believing is seeing"* is a more appropriate way to put it for the genuine Christian. Put your security where it belongs, and the rest of these things will lessen in importance in your life.

Misplaced Trust

Back in 1923, some of the wealthiest and most notable businessmen in the United States got together at the Edgewater Beach Hotel in Chicago (the press reported they were there to divide the country up amongst themselves). Among those gathered were the president of the largest independent steel company, the president of National City Bank, the president of the nation's largest utility company, the president of the largest gas company, the country's greatest wheat baron, the president of the New York Stock Exchange, a member of the president's cabinet, and head of the Bank of International Settlements.

Twenty-six years later, Charles Schwab died bankrupt, Samuel Insull died as a fugitive running from justice, Howard Hopson was insane, Arthur Cotton died a poor man having fled the U.S., Richard Whitney had just been released from prison, Albert Fall had just received a pardon from prison so he could go home to die, Jesse Livermore and Leon Fraser had committed suicide. The most powerful and some of the wealthiest men in the country were in ruins or dead not too long after the much hyped meeting in Chicago.

Wealth tends to change a man, so God has much to say about it—**"The rich man's wealth is his fortress, the ruin of the poor is their poverty"** (10:15). Let's take this Proverb a phrase at a time.

"The rich man's wealth is his fortress." Although most of the Proverbs have a positive and negative side to them, this one really doesn't. This phrase in verse 15 may seem to have some positive qualities (and, from a worldly point of view, it does), but it is actually a rebuke. It's a rebuke to those who put their trust in riches. Yes, there are many advantages afforded to those who have money, because money can buy a lot of things and money can get you out of many kinds of difficult circumstances—but it should not be where your trust is placed.

A preacher once preached a sermon reciting from the Scripture that nothing really belongs to us. A very wealthy man who heard the sermon invited the preacher over for lunch that afternoon. After their meal together, he walked the preacher around his estate pointing out all the buildings and land and cars and possessions he owned. He then turned to the preacher and said, *"You said this morning that these things do not belong to me—I beg to differ. These are all mine."* The preacher simply responded, *"Tell me again about what you own in a hundred years."*

Psalm 52:7 speaks to this attitude of trusting in wealth—**"Behold, the man who would not make God his refuge, but trusted in the abundance of his riches and was strong in his evil desire."** Those who trust in riches have no need for God—or at least they think they have no need for God.

"The ruin of the poor is their poverty." The last phrase of this Proverb simply states the plight of those who live in poverty. It is a rare thing for one to escape the clutches of poverty. There is very little opportunity afforded to the poor to improve his or her station in life. It's almost as if there are physical barriers surrounding the ghettos of our nation's major cities—not barriers to keep people from getting in, but barriers to keep those who live there from getting out.

Jesus says that we will always have the poor with us, but He also showed us by His actions and His words that we should help the poor, especially if you have been blessed with wealth. And, quite honestly, compared with 90% or more of this world's population, if you are reading this, you are wealthy.

Be wise in your use of this wealth God has blessed you with by, first, not placing your security in it. But there's more on this issue.

Be brutally honest with yourself and answer these questions: Who do you trust? Or, in what do you trust?

Most Christians would probably automatically say they trust God, but, if you dig a little deeper, you will find in most cases they really don't. They may want to, and their soul may long to place their complete trust in God, but their trust usually will end up in something or someone tangible in their own mind. They have taken the phrase, *"God helps those who help themselves"* and turned it into a biblical mandate. That phrase is not biblical at all, it actually goes totally against the principles of the Bible. All throughout the Scripture, we see that God helps those who cannot help themselves (this is true even of our salvation).

Solomon adds to this issue of false security or false trust with one of the wrong things to place your trust in—**"He who trusts in his riches will fall"** (11:28a). This will hit most Christians where it hurts. It doesn't matter how much or how little money you have, most Christians place their trust in the almighty dollar. You may be saying right now, *"You're wrong, Al."* And I hope that I am, but hear me out and take a hard look at yourself and your finances.

As Americans, we have been so blessed by God that we really do not understand money very well. The things we look at as necessities are luxuries in most other nations and cultures around this world. Again, do not get me wrong as there is absolutely nothing unbiblical about having the riches of this world. Many of the great characters we look to in the Scripture were some of the wealthiest men of their time—Abraham, Isaac, Jacob, Job, Solomon, David, etc. The issue we must struggle with, especially in America, is how we use these riches and what place they hold in our lives.

A missionary friend of mine in Nepal sent me a Thanksgiving email, praising God for America because of missionaries who were sent from the U.S. to bring the gospel message to his country. Let me share with you a portion of his letter in the broken English in which he wrote:

> *Our ancestors were naked; hungered without food, illiterate, headhunters, and all the time fear of evil spirit, and were trying please the evil spirit to escape from the harm. While they were in the midst of darkness, the American missionaries brought the light of Jesus to the Nagas in 1872. As we received the light, the headhunters turn into soul hunters. Today there are many Naga missionaries working all over the world. It is the fruit of American missionaries.*

American Christians have been financially blessed beyond measure in comparison to most of the world. Jesus said, **"From everyone who has been given much, much will be required; and to whom they entrusted much, of him they will ask all the more"** (Luke 12:48b). Most Christians look upon the finances they have received from the Lord as their own possession, to spend as they please on what Madison Avenue tells us we need. Most Christians do not understand the responsibility they have to evangelize the world (Acts 1:8; Matthew 28:19–20) and how the finances God entrusts to our care can be used for such a great commission; a commission that has been given to us, been commanded to us. A portion of these finances could be used by supporting those who are taking the gospel message to the masses in this country and throughout the world.

Again, my point today is not to make you feel guilty for what you have, but to make you think and to seek God in how you use the resources He has supplied. For when you do follow His leading in this area, and when you do entirely put your trust in Him, you can claim the last part of our Proverb today—**"But the righteous will flourish like the green leaf"**

(11:28b). Or, you can be self-deceived by allowing your trust and security to be placed in paper dollars.

False Impressions

Looks can be deceiving. I heard the following story from a Steve Brown sermon:

> A taxi driver in New York City picked up a nun. He turned to the nun and said, "I am so excited that I finally have a nun in my taxi. I have always wanted to ... I'm sorry, I can't."
>
> The nun replied, "No, go ahead—what did you want to say?"
>
> The taxi driver replied, "Well, I have always wanted to kiss a nun, but I know that's probably not possible.
>
> The nun said, "If you are Catholic and you are single, it's okay."
>
> The taxi driver excitedly exclaimed, "I am Catholic, and I am single."
>
> The nun said, "Pull over."
>
> He did so and leaned back and gave the nun a big old kiss. As he pulled away from the curb, he said, "I feel so guilty now." When the nun asked why, he replied, "I'm actually a Protestant and I'm married."
>
> The nun said, "That's okay, my name is Charlie and I'm on my way to a costume party."

Pretending to be someone you are not and thus making a false impression is the lesson in this next Proverb—**"Better is he who is lightly esteemed and has a servant than he who honors himself and lacks bread"** (12:9). People are always trying to impress others, even if it means being a hypocrite. At the different stages of a person's life, there are certain items one seemingly must possess to maintain social status.

For me, as a teenager, I had to have a killer stereo system (something I somewhat still desire even today). My very first foray into the world of buying on credit was for a cassette deck when I was eighteen. For you, it may have been something different. I've known people who have to have certain types of cars or trucks—not for the practical aspect but for the social status it brings. I saw an elderly lady (she had to be at least eighty) driving a Porsche Boxster at a Walmart recently, parking it at the very back of the parking lot and hiking her way ever so slowly to the store entrance. Now if she can afford a Porsche, I guess there is nothing wrong with owning one. It just doesn't seem to be the most practical vehicle for an elderly woman—and you just don't see too many Porsche cars in the Walmart parking lot.

Watch the next television ad you see for a car; the ads never tell you anything about the car itself, but instead simply tries to make you want the car for the false status it can bring you.

Those who purchase things for the status usually can't afford the item—they just want people to think they can afford it. These are the people Solomon is talking about **who honors himself and lacks bread**. They spend the resources God gives them trying to impress other people while ignoring the necessities of life.

I once owned a lawn and landscape business in the suburbs of Chicago, but I did not have a plow truck (most in this industry would plow snow during the winter months). So, instead of plowing snow, I picked up odd jobs including delivering pizzas. There was a very exclusive neighborhood close to the pizza place I delivered for. It was a relatively new development and the houses were much larger and expensive than the surrounding neighborhoods. The first time I had a pizza delivery in that neighborhood, I got excited thinking I would get a sizable tip, but I was wrong. It was indeed a huge fancy house and there was an expensive car in the driveway, but the house was almost empty. As I drove away with virtually no tip, I noticed, up and down the streets, other fancy homes with very little furniture. It was a neighborhood of big houses and fancy cars the affluent would own, but these folks apparently were not in that social class. They lived in almost empty houses for the status of their address.

Solomon says, "**Better is he who is lightly esteemed and has a servant.**" By **lightly esteemed**, he simply means someone who is not looked upon as someone of wealth or social status. Most of you know that Sam Walton was this way. Mr. Walton (founder of Walmart) drove around in an old, dented pickup truck and wore faded blue jeans, yet he was one of the wealthiest men in the entire world. If you did not know what he looked like, you would pass by him without a second thought as to him being wealthy and of importance. And that is much better than falsely gaining someone's attention and going hungry.

Jesus tells us to not show partiality to others because of their wealth or social status, so we definitely should not let our pride drive us to want that treatment from others. God made you uniquely. He doesn't make mistakes. Be who you are. Be genuine. It's better that way.

Dream Mentality

Hope. The word hope is powerful. When we have hope in any given situation, we are motivated to keep on keeping on. When a situation we face is hopeless, we become depressed, despondent, and somewhat emotionally paralyzed. From the secular definition of the word, hope is something that does not have an assured outcome but only a possible outcome (i.e. "*I hope the economy turns around soon*"). From the biblical definition, hope is something that is assured without any doubt ("*Jesus Christ is the **hope of our salvation***"). In either case, hope spurs us on while the lack of hope demoralizes us.

When we focus our thoughts on the future, everyone lives with a certain measure of hope that things will get better. We may have goals to eliminate our debt, or improve our health through diet and exercise, or develop new skills that make our services in the working world more marketable, or grow spiritually through the discipline of spending more time in Bible study, etc. I don't know anyone who does not want their lives to be progressively better in one or many ways. The hope for a better future is common to all of us. Even those who do not appear to show any hope for tomorrow prove they do by continuing to get out of bed each morning.

Solomon does not want to destroy our hope for the future, but he does want us to reorient our thinking—**"Do not boast about tomorrow, for you do not know what a day may bring forth"** (27:1).

A great quote from an unidentified author fits the main point—*"Yesterday is history and tomorrow is a mystery; today is a gift, that's why it is called the present."* The obvious point is that we must always live our lives in the present moment. We cannot change the past and we are not guaranteed that our hearts will continue to beat beyond this moment, let alone ten, twenty, or thirty years into the future, so we only have right now. The question then is, what are you doing with your life right now? What is your attitude right now? How is your life impacting other people right now? What are you doing that has eternal significance right now?

I want to eliminate all of my personal debt. I want to lose weight and have more energy. I want to spend more time in deep study of God's Word. I want to spend more time in prayer and communion and fellowship and intimate relationship with the Lord. I would venture to guess that several of these personal desires of mine are the same personal desires for you, but the problem is that most of us are looking at these "dreams" as something that will happen in the future. And, for most of us, they really are only dreams because we are not doing anything to realize these desires right now.

This dream mentality is one of the most devious tricks of Satan because dreams are all about tomorrow. Of course, we are to have visions of tomorrow and we are to make plans for the future as long as we keep the Lord in the loop, but, if we are not doing anything today to move toward these dreams and plans, then they are nothing more than dreams and plans; they are a waste of our energy. Tomorrow is not a guarantee to any of us; the only thing that matters is right now. Solomon is urging us to get our heads out of the clouds and to focus on right now.

It took me far too long to embrace this attitude. I was a dreamer in this respect. The above goals I listed were always just dreams that I had deceived myself into thinking they would somehow magically take place without any significant change on my part. Now, I have plans of action that I am working on every day to realize these goals—they are not dreams anymore, they are realities that are getting progressively closer to being fulfilled. But I had to change. I had to take advantage of today instead of only dreaming about tomorrow.

So, in the midst of your job or your daily responsibilities or whatever else your routine includes, take a moment to reorient your thinking. Praise God for this moment in time. Thank Him for this day. Then take advantage of the time you have right now to make the improvements in your life that have, up until now, been stuck in the fantasy that is tomorrow.

* * *

TAKE ACTION

I implore you to pay attention at this moment! I can tell you from my experience and from the overwhelming evidence of human nature that this one action step will determine if this book will be of any benefit to you at all. You must realize that your good intentions are absolutely worthless! Unless you resist the urge to continue reading and stop to take the time to figure out how you will follow through with any valuable nugget of information that resonates with you, this is an exercise in futility. I commend you for investing your time and money into the reading of this book, but, without follow through, it will just be more information being crammed into your overstuffed brain.

What step are you going to take right now? Write it down, and take at least one positive action toward your pursuit before continuing your reading.

CHAPTER 9

Pulling Weeds

God invented weeds as part of the curse for sin, and so they should be an ever-present reminder of the pervasive impact of sin. Some weeds are thorny and prickly, some are noxious and poisonous, some will wrap around healthy plants and choke the life out of them, and some disguise themselves as pretty flowers, but all will spread and wreak havoc on a yard, garden, or a field of crops if not dealt with severely.

The battle with weeds is never-ending. The moment you think you have won, the child next door picks a fuzzy dandelion and blows the seeds to the wind—which, of course, is heading in your direction as, seemingly in slow motion, you dive in front of the onslaught like a secret service agent protecting the president, yelling, "Noooooooooo!"

Weeds are everywhere, both literally and figuratively. As you begin (or continue) this journey to get your financial garden growing and flourishing, there are many weeds to be aware of; they must be quickly exterminated. Some of the weeds are obvious, such as compromise, envy, and arrogance, but others are subtler, such as social status, favoritism, and phoniness. All weeds can creep in unawares and do damage, and eventually overwhelm and destroy.

Let's see what wisdom can be found to help us pull some weeds.

Compromise

"My son, if sinners entice you, do not consent. If they say, 'Come with us, let us lie in wait for blood, let us ambush the innocent without cause; let us swallow them alive like Sheol, even whole, as those who go down to the pit; we will find all kinds of precious wealth, we will fill our houses with spoil; throw in your lot with us, we shall have one purse,' my son, do not walk in the way with them. Keep your feet from their path, for their feet run to evil and they hasten to shed blood. Indeed, it is useless to spread the baited net in the sight of any bird; but they lie in wait for their own blood; they ambush their own lives. So are the ways of everyone who gains by violence; it takes away the life of its possessors" (1:10–19).

In the movie *Wall Street* with Michael Douglas and Charlie Sheen, the character played by Douglas (Gordon Gekko) says, "*Greed, for lack of a better word, is good. Greed is right. Greed works. Greed clarifies and cuts through and captures the essence of evolutionary spirit. Greed in all of its forms, greed for life, for money, for love, and knowledge has marked the upward surge of mankind.*"

Gekko was a multi-millionaire who made most of his money through hostile takeovers of companies by buying controlling interest of their stock. He always targeted the companies he would takeover by getting "inside information," which is an illegal practice. Gekko entices the character played by Sheen (Bud Fox) to join him and get the inside information he needed on the companies he had interest in.

Initially Fox resists—he had never before done anything illegal in his profession as a stock broker. But, eventually, Gekko wears Fox down with his offer of untold wealth and the lifestyle and perks that it would bring. As the money starts pouring in, Fox's conscience becomes dull to the illegal activities he continues to participate in. He is blinded and consumed by the lifestyle he now lives.

Solomon warns us of the dangers of getting involved with people like Gordon Gekko, because the temptation to compromise is too great for most to resist. Solomon tells us to not even be in the same vicinity of those who do such mischief. Don't associate with them and don't even hang around them.

Oh, how tempting it is to grab a little of this world's goods in the wrong way. You can begin to rationalize your actions. Someone shows you how to get away with cheating on your taxes, or how to get free Internet TV, or … you fill in the blanks. We must not even entertain the thought, for it is in the mind where sin is first committed. The actual activity of the sin is secondary, but it will follow once it has been implanted in the mind. Jesus says that once the thought is being cultivated and considered and imagined in your mind, you have already committed the sin (Matthew 5:21–30).

When you reach for wealth and this world's goods in the wrong way, you are destroying your own life. All that glitters is not gold. Those who pursue gain through illegal or immoral or compromised means will ultimately pay for their crimes, even if they seemingly get away with such in the society—temporarily.

The weed of compromise is subtle and insidious. Doing the right thing will sometimes cause more immediate problems than compromise, so it seems like the right and just thing to do is avoid the trouble. But you simply can't. Following the morals and justifications of the world and expecting divine blessing is ludicrous. Cutting corners in your financial life because "everyone else is doing it" is a horrible plan. You must not join in with the crowd, no matter how enticing and no matter how small the odds are to get caught. Compromise kills and destroys and ruins; if not outwardly, it will slowly and painfully eat away at you inwardly.

In the movie, both Gekko and Fox go to prison for their crimes even though Fox tries to do the right thing and make up for his illegal activity. In real life, not all crooks get caught by the society, but all is seen by God; absolutely nothing escapes His watchful eye (Hebrews 4:13); and God's justice and judgment is eventually and ultimately meted out with no exceptions.

Take Solomon's advice and run away from those who scheme and plot, so that you do not even have a chance to let it begin to germinate in your mind.

Envy

Do you remember a man by the name of Robin Leach? He was the host of a television program called *Lifestyles of the Rich and Famous*. He took you through the houses and yachts and private jets of movie stars and rock stars and wealthy business owners. During its day, this was a very popular program. Today, there are many daily programs all over the airwaves following the lives of the rich and famous—there is even an entire channel devoted to nothing but this, twenty-four hours a day. Most watch these programs to escape from their "normal" mundane lives, and dream about what it would be like trade places with the stars. Others become obsessed and try to be like the people they idolize.

Solomon has a warning for us in this next Proverb—**"Do not envy a man of violence and do not choose any of his ways"** (3:31). Although I won't go as far as to say that the rich and famous are people of violence (not all of them anyway), their lifestyles could rarely be called godly. The word translated as **"violence"** has a deeper meaning in the original Hebrew than our English word conveys. It can also imply one who oppresses another, or one who does evil for his own profit, or one who climbs to the top by any means necessary—even if he steps on others along the way. This attitude is common among those who are desperately trying to reach the same level of fame and fortune of these celebrities.

This Proverb warns us to not choose any of their ways. Do not mimic their philosophy. Stop agreeing with their point of view. Don't get caught up in the fantasy world of desiring to be like them. God created you for a special and specific purpose in this life, and it has nothing to do with the world's standard of celebrity and success.

Psalm 73 has tremendous value and wisdom for us when we feel sorry for ourselves and begin to envy those who seem to prosper while living a godless life. I encourage you to read it often.

Fame and fortune will fade away. There is no lasting or eternal value to being rich or famous. God may indeed allow you to become wealthy—the Scripture tells us that God gives us the power to make wealth (Deuteronomy 8:18), but it does not say we should pursue wealth for the sake of being rich.

As for fame, God may also indeed allow you to be famous in some way, but the pursuit of fame is totally against God's principle of humility. Our lives should reflect the attitude of John the Baptist when he said, "**He must increase, but I must decrease**" (John 3:30). John was a celebrity of sorts in his time, it just wasn't a status he pursued, and he was quick to let go of that status to exalt Christ.

God has strong words for people who pursue their own gain by ungodly means or for ungodly purposes—"**For the devious are an abomination to the LORD**" (3:32a). Which begs the question for us, "Am I willing to pursue riches and fame at the expense of being **an abomination to the Lord?** An abomination is something detestable and despised. Think of something that you despise—is that how you want God to feel about your actions? Then do not envy them or copy their ways. Live a godly life and enjoy the relationship with God that He has designed and desired—"**but He is intimate with the upright**" (3:32b).

The lifestyles of the rich and famous may look desirable. It may seem as if they have everything you want—but it is all an illusion. Here is Psalm 73—I think you will identify with the writer and I trust you will come to the same conclusion:

> "**Surely God is good to Israel,**
> > **To those who are pure in heart!**
> **But as for me, my feet came close to stumbling,**
> > **My steps had almost slipped.**
> **For I was envious of the arrogant**
> > **As I saw the prosperity of the wicked.**
> **For there are no pains in their death,**
> > **And their body is fat.**

They are not in trouble as other men,
Nor are they plagued like mankind.
Therefore pride is their necklace;
The garment of violence covers them.
Their eye bulges from fatness;
The imaginations of their heart run riot.
They mock and wickedly speak of oppression;
They speak from on high.
They have set their mouth against the heavens,
And their tongue parades through the earth.
Therefore his people return to this place,
And waters of abundance are drunk by them.
They say, 'How does God know?
And is there knowledge with the Most High?'
Behold, these are the wicked;
And always at ease, they have increased in wealth.
Surely in vain I have kept my heart pure
And washed my hands in innocence;
For I have been stricken all day long
And chastened every morning.

If I had said, 'I will speak thus,'
Behold, I would have betrayed the generation of Your
children.
When I pondered to understand this,
It was troublesome in my sight
Until I came into the sanctuary of God;
Then I perceived their end.
Surely You set them in slippery places;
You cast them down to destruction.
How they are destroyed in a moment!
They are utterly swept away by sudden terrors!
Like a dream when one awakes,

O Lord, when aroused, You will despise their form.
When my heart was embittered
    And I was pierced within,
Then I was senseless and ignorant;
    I was like a beast before You.
Nevertheless I am continually with You;
    You have taken hold of my right hand.
With Your counsel You will guide me,
    And afterward receive me to glory.
Whom have I in heaven but You?
    And besides You, I desire nothing on earth.
My flesh and my heart may fail,
    But God is the strength of my heart and my portion forever.
For, behold, those who are far from You will perish;
    You have destroyed all those who are unfaithful to You.
But as for me, the nearness of God is my good;
    I have made the Lord God my refuge,
    That I may tell of all Your works."

Outward Appearances and Phoniness

"The curse of the Lord is on the house of the wicked, but He blesses the dwelling of the righteous" (3:33). The two words translated here as house and dwelling have significance based on the context of the passage. The great Puritan commentator, Matthew Henry, comments on this implication in the text:

> "The wicked has a house, a strong and stately dwelling perhaps, but the curse of the Lord is upon it, and, though the affairs of the family may prosper, yet the very blessings are curses. There is leanness in the soul. The curse may work silently and slowly; but it is as a fretting leprosy; it will consume the timber thereof and the stones thereof. The just have a habitation, a poor cottage, a very mean dwelling; but God blesses it; he is

continually blessing it, from the beginning of the year to the end of it. The curse or blessing of God is upon the house according as the inhabitants are wicked or godly; and it is certain that a blessed family, though poor, has no reason to envy a cursed family, though rich."

It is infinitely better to have the blessing of God yet have simple possessions and means than to have the curse of God and dwell in material prosperity. This verse does not mean that all who are wealthy are cursed and all who are poor are blessed, nor vice versa. The blessing and the curse come based upon the heart of the person. And based upon a righteous heart, if the choice was laid before you, the wise choice is God's blessing even if it means simple living or even poverty.

This brings us one more point—the blessing of God doesn't necessarily have anything to do with your level of wealth or lack thereof. I consider my father to be one of the most blessed men I have ever known, yet he has never had much of this world's goods. But he has a family that serves God. His children and grandchildren know the Lord—is there really any greater blessing than that?

Take a step back and reevaluate the blessings God has given you. Don't look at the outside or the things you have, but rather look on the inside. The outside can fool you, but outward appearances can cut both ways.

Putting on a good appearance smacks too much of being phony to me. I know appearances are important (especially first appearances), and I know that we all will modify our appearance when going to a wedding or funeral or some other social event, but it can become too easy to put on a false front if you fall into the habit of always making yourself appear different than you really are. The outward phoniness can creep its way inside. I am a jeans, T-shirt, and flannel kind of guy. I don't mind dressing up when the occasion calls for it, but, all things being equal, I would much rather be who I am instead of pretending to be someone different.

Please understand I am not saying that dressing nice makes you a phony. Dressing nice is a requirement with some occupations, and, for some people, it is indeed who they really are. What I am attempting to say is the way you dress says a lot about you, and, if you get to the point where you are afraid to let anyone see the real you—meaning that you can't even force yourself to go to the grocery store unless you are all dressed up and made up (in essence, worried about how others will view you), then you are dangerously close to crossing the line into phoniness.

In the '70s and '80s (and, to a lesser extent, still today), the television evangelists and their wives and associates would help me make my point. The makeup and the outfits they wore just oozed with phoniness—and many of them were eventually exposed to be just that. Of course, you should be dressed nicely if you have a television ministry, but there is a difference between being nicely dressed and oozing phoniness.

This next Proverb deals with the fact that phoniness will eventually be exposed—**"The crown of the wise is their riches, but the folly of fools is foolishness"** (14:24).

At first glance, you may think this Proverb is speaking about riches and wealth, but that is not the focal point. Solomon is speaking about how our internal qualities can be hidden for only so long. The focus of the Proverb is the same as so many others; it is comparing and contrasting the wise with the foolish. The wealth of wisdom and, by the same standard, the poverty of foolishness will eventually be exposed in the life of the person. It will be as evident as wearing a crown.

If a person walked down Main Street in your town wearing a crown, it would be noticed by all who even glanced in their direction. So, too, will the godly wisdom or the worldly foolishness you possess. You cannot hide who you truly are forever; eventually, it will be plain and obvious to everyone who sees you.

The wonderful part of this is that you don't have to be phony nor do you have to stay the way you are—you can change! If you do not possess a lot of godly wisdom, you can start obtaining it right now. If you do not know your Bible very well, you can start knowing it better today. If you do not understand all the intricacies of finance and handling your money, you can easily correct that now (as you are obviously starting). If you are lacking in other areas of knowledge and wisdom, you can begin increasing your knowledge and wisdom at this moment. You do not have to remain where you are—you can make the necessary changes in your life to scale greater heights. But you must make the effort.

If you keep doing what you have always been doing, you will keep getting what you have always been getting. It is insanity, as they say, to think your results will change when your actions do not. No amount of wishing and hoping changes a single thing. Your actions must be in pursuit of genuine change, though, not simply for the sake of appearances.

Don't be a phony—you can only hide the real you for so long anyway. Most people catch on to your game much quicker you think. If you don't like the real you, then get busy making the necessary changes to become the masterpiece God designed you to be! Don't settle for mediocre, pull that weed!

Injustice – Favoritism

Who do you try to impress? Are there people out there whom you will go out of your way to do things for? Do you seek opportunities to honor those to whom honor is due?

Unfortunately, most people are primarily focused on themselves. Your position in society, the college degrees you may have earned through disciplined study and long hours, and even the authority you may have earned on the job through hard work and years of service don't receive much notice by those around you. Not that you achieved any of this so people would notice you, but the point is that most do not honor the achievement and accomplishment of others. Most are so self-engrossed that honor is not bestowed on those to whom honor is due—and, tragically, this has spilled over into Christianity. Even God is hardly honored by most Christians.

Case in point, this next Proverb tells us one simple way that we honor God, yet most Christians are rarely, if ever, involved in any activities that show this type of honor—**"He who oppresses the poor taunts his Maker, but he who is gracious to the needy honors Him"** (14:31). I would guess that most Christians are not knowingly involved in oppressing the poor, but very few are actively involved in helping them.

Helping the poor is an impossible task to ever complete. Poverty will never be eliminated until this age ends. It is an impossible task. Jesus Himself said, "**For you always have the poor with you**" (Matthew 26:11). But even though there will be a never-ending line of people who live in poverty across this globe, that does not negate our responsibility to help when God places the need before us.

James 2:14–17 tells us, "**What use is it, my brethren, if someone says he has faith but he has no works? Can that faith save him? If a brother or sister is without clothing and in need of daily food, and one of you says to them, 'Go in peace, be warmed and be filled,' and yet you do not give them what is necessary for their body, what use is that? Even so faith, if it has no works, is dead, being by itself.**"

In the context of the passage in James, when we choose to not help our Christian brothers and sisters who are struggling to put food on the table and keep the heat and electricity on, we are indeed oppressing the poor (sometimes that help includes education if their plight is due to habitually poor choices). And, more importantly, when we choose to ignore these needs, we are taunting God. When we ignore God's command to help the poor and needy, we might as well be looking God in the face and hurling insults at Him.

On the other hand, when we choose to help those whom God places in our path, we are heaping honor upon our Heavenly Father. We are honoring the One who has allowed us to have so much. But, by the grace of God, you could be the one who has no food and little clothing and no place to live.

Wow! That's something to think about. But don't think too long—is there really a choice when it comes to either insulting or honoring our God and King? Solomon has more to say about the weeds of injustice and favoritism.

It wasn't very long ago when I was exposed to the concept of a peanut butter and banana sandwich. At the time, I was working with a gentleman in our church who ran his own lawn and landscape business. We stopped for lunch one day and he was eating one of these delicacies that his wife had packed for him. Apparently, this concoction is an invention of those who live in the South, and while my folks are from what some consider the South, they are not Deep South. My initial reaction was, *"Oh, that just isn't right!"* But I then realized that I like peanut butter, I like bananas, and I like bread. So, I tried one when I got home that evening and was forever hooked.

While it turns out that peanut butter and banana sandwiches are all right (at least according to my tastes now), there are things in this world that are simply not right (like anything with broccoli). Solomon speaks of two such instances in this next Proverb—**"Luxury is not fitting for a fool; much less for a slave to rule over princes"** (19:10).

Fools simply should not live in luxury. A fool, in the sense of Proverbs, is not necessarily someone who is mentally challenged, but someone who chooses laziness over hard work, who shuns additional learning, who rejects wisdom and the advice of others, who ignores his or her conscience, and who lacks initiative, etc. A person with these character traits should not enjoy the benefits of luxurious accommodations or a lifestyle of plenty. It just isn't right in the moral order of things.

A slave or servant simply should not have authority over royalty. It upsets the apple cart. Servants are hired to serve royalty—it's just that simple.

So, what is Solomon telling us? What application can we draw out of these obvious statements?

I offer you this: Even though there are things in this world that simply should not be, sometimes they are. Injustices happen every day all over this world. How do you handle them when they affect you? Do you let them ruin your day? Do they disrupt your focus? Do you question how God could let these things happen?

Bad things happen in this world. Not a single one of them happen apart from God's allowance, so we must understand that God has a purpose in allowing injustice for a season. Did it ever occur to you that nothing ever occurs to God? Absolutely nothing happens apart from God allowing it to happen. There is not a single rogue atom or molecule that is off doing its own thing. This does not mean that God is the author of the evil that happens, it only means that He allows it for His ultimate divine purposes of which we know nothing about.

This weed of injustice has two sides to it. First, we cannot be a participant in being unjust with anybody or in any of our dealings, whether personal or business related. But, secondly, we must understand and even expect that injustices will occur, and, sometimes, we are going to be on the receiving end.

You may embrace the focus of this book and resolve to study God's principles of handling money, you may not only study but diligently apply everything you learn, and you may make this change of thinking a true change in lifestyle, but you could still be a victim of an injustice that negatively impacts your finances. Stay the course anyway—God eventually settles all accounts.

So, the next time you see something that just isn't right, don't fret. God is still on the throne and He knows about it. Don't let it ruin your day or cause you to question God. Just thank God that He is in control and continue on the path God has given you.

And you must try a peanut butter and banana sandwich!

But the weed of injustice can still be a problem. And we must be diligent and cautious to not get drawn into allowing it to even briefly enter our mind.

There is much injustice in the world today—always has been and always will be, until Jesus Christ returns and sets up His Kingdom on this earth. All you have to do is pick up a newspaper or turn on the news and you will see account after account across the globe of that which is unjust. Millions of children go to sleep every night with swollen bellies from hunger pains, through no fault of their own. Innocent people are kidnapped, held hostage, and usually executed just because they happened to be in the wrong place at the wrong time. Men, women, and children are torn apart by roadside bombs for no humane reason. Unborn babies are slaughtered by the millions just because their mothers and fathers don't want them inconveniencing their lives. Hard-working people lose their jobs and their retirement money because of the greed of others—usually with no recourse. You get the picture.

Injustice is the topic of yet another Proverb—**"Abundant food is in the fallow ground of the poor, but it is swept away by injustice"** (13:23). The injustices of this world are almost exclusively perpetrated upon those who do not have the means or ability to fight back. The poor farmer may be able to work hard enough to see his land produce crops for his family and to earn a meager living, but it can all disappear in a heartbeat. There is always someone who will take advantage of the poor and the helpless.

You see this even in the banks, mortgage companies, finance companies, and insurance companies today. Those who have fallen on hard times and struggle making ends meet pay higher interest rates and higher premiums than those who have plenty of money. The rich have choices, so the world caters to them. The poor are left with paying the tab in a take it or leave it market place.

Although it may seem as if injustice abounds, God is keeping track of all that happens, and all accounts will be settled. God is perfectly just. No injustice escapes His sight and those who have unjustly suffered will receive their "day in court," so to speak.

So, what do we do with this information? There does not appear to be a command for us in this Proverb, it just looks like Solomon is making a statement of fact. How do we apply this to our lives?

James 1:27 tells us, **"Pure and undefiled religion in the sight of our God and Father is this: to visit orphans and widows in their distress, and to keep oneself unstained by the world."** We apply our Proverb by paying attention and acting on the behalf of those who are facing injustice. Contribute to food pantries or start one yourself, actively and consistently pray for those who are held hostage and those who live in war-torn countries, fight for the unborn, buy a bag of groceries for your neighbor who lost his job, etc. God has left it for us to help those around us when we are able. In the end, as we already said, God will make things right. But, in the meantime, it is our duty to do what we can.

One of the responsibilities we all have, as we get our finances in order according to the Scripture, is to be generous and help others with the abundance God provides; and I can speak from experience of how God indeed provides when we make the genuine effort to follow His principles, precepts, and commands concerning money.

Show mercy and grace to those who face injustice—after all, we have received the ultimate mercy and grace from our Savior.

Arrogance

Arrogance is ugly. Arrogance is presumptive. Arrogance is prideful. And arrogance is not confined to the wealthy, the famous, or the social elite. You can be destitute and be arrogant. You can be invisible to the world and be arrogant. You can be young or old, short or tall, fat or skinny, red or yellow, black or white, educated or illiterate, male or female, believer or unbeliever—anyone can be arrogant. And it is still ugly regardless of the source.

This last weed we will cover in this chapter may look innocent enough on the surface, but this Proverb strikes at the core of an ugly problem that haunts us all at one time or another—**"The rich and the poor have a common bond, the LORD is the maker of them all"** (22:2).

Many years ago, I was sitting in traffic on a suburban Chicago street. Life was good. I was involved in ministry as much or more than a layperson could be. I was a deacon in my church, I was the worship leader, the choir director; I sang solos, duets, and was the bass in a church quartet. I taught an adult Sunday school class and a Bible study. I was disciplining a young couple, and I was even referred to as Pastor Al by some in the church well before God called me to be a pastor. As I said, life was good.

While waiting for the traffic light to turn green, an older model car pulled up alongside of me with some Hispanic polka style music blaring. I was in a large pickup truck at the time, so my seating position was elevated in comparison to this car. The irony didn't hit me right away because it happened so quickly. I turned and literally looked down on the car beside me, and then, in my heart, I looked down on the person inside the car. I felt disdain for this person because of the annoying music he was blaring so proudly.

Immediately, God struck me for my atrocious sin. Prior to that experience, I would have defended myself to the grave that I did not have a prejudice or arrogant bone in my body. But, in a single moment of time, God reached deep into my soul and exposed an ugly cancer within. Who was I to look down on anybody? It was only by the grace of God that I was able to do or be anything. It was only by God's allowance that I was able to serve in the church. It was only by God's providence that I was born in the affluence and opulence that is the United States of America, instead of the poverty and disease of a third world country.

God made each and every person who has ever set foot on this earth. How arrogant is it when we look down on any of His creation? And this happens even amongst believers. The Apostle Paul had to deal with this in his epistle to the Romans—"**Who are you to judge the servant of another?**" meaning another servant of God (Romans 14:4a). Paul's question was directed at the spiritually mature who were looking down on those who had not yet reached their level of understanding in Christian freedom and liberty. These immature Christians were still stuck in traditionalism. They still refused to eat certain foods and they still regarded certain days as more holy than others, but God was not condemning these for their immaturity, He was condemning the spiritually mature for being arrogant.

As you progress in your knowledge, wisdom, understanding, and application of God's principles in finance, you will receive the blessing of increase. If you are not cognizant of this trap, it will be insanely easy to allow the weed of arrogance to take root; you may not even realize it until the first time you catch yourself looking down on others who squander what little money they have.

God brought me to tears on that day as I sat in traffic, tears of disgust and tears of repentance.

Arrogance is ugly. Ask God to rid you of this weed each and every time it appears in your life, whether you are rich and look down on the poor or are poor and look with disdain at the rich. Our common bond is God created us all—and He does not make mistakes.

It is a never-ending battle with weeds, so become excellent at recognizing them and eradicating them.

* * *

TAKE ACTION

We all have weeds in our life. Write down the ones that need attention and get busy. Do additional research, read some more, ask for advice, then do the hard work to pull those pesky weeds that want nothing more than to destroy your future.

CHAPTER 10

MISS THESE AND YOU HAVE MISSED EVERYTHING (PART 1)

Since the advent of social media, I have witnessed the tendency we have of zoning in on pieces of information or opinions that are posted, often completely missing the point being made. I can write a post of several paragraphs on a very specific topic, yet get all kinds of blowback on an insignificant phrase contained in the post. And often, the phrase that is misused and abused is then twisted to contradict my intent.

If we do not resolve to employ caution, we will only see what we want to see. This habit or lack in our observational skills can cause undue pain and unnecessary frustration. When self-imposed blinders block our sight to all the pertinent information, we can sabotage the potential positive impact of true knowledge and wisdom by eliminating a key step or essential component.

In Christianity, for example, we can be laser-focused on seeing people come to Christ in genuine conversion—and that's terrific. But, if that is all you see and choose to skip the biblical mandate to make disciples, the new converts will be left to survive on their own, which likely means they will never grow in their faith and be easy prey for the enemy.

I once attended a church that set a goal to see 500 souls make a profession of faith each year, and, for three years straight, we supposedly reached that goal. The problem was, our attendance did not grow hardly at all in those three years—where were those 1,500 people? It's possible that some were never truly converted, but it is more likely that we simply skipped biblical discipleship by choosing to not see that vital role we are called to fulfill.

The depth of wisdom that Solomon has for us in the Book of Proverbs is immense. And while I have been attempting to point out and somewhat single out the ones that pertain to handling our finances, we really cannot separate things quite that succinctly. We cannot just choose to follow only Proverbs that deal with increasing money and expect our finances to prosper. We must also grasp and absorb and apply the myriad other principles that will transform us into the man or woman whom God can trust with money—not from the perspective of misusing the money, but because of the real danger that an abundance of money could expose us to.

So, in these closing chapters, we must embrace what Solomon (and other writers in Proverbs) have to teach us concerning our attitudes and actions. Only as we internalize these principles, will we be prepared for the challenge and blessing of God's increased provision.

Attitudes

When young children are in your home, when do you suddenly get concerned about what they are doing? When our kids were young, it was rare to not hear some kind of noise or commotion at all times. Sometimes laughter, sometimes crying, sometimes the TV, sometimes furniture falling over, etc., but there was always some noise. When things got too quiet, we became concerned—and, more often than not, the quiet indicated that one or both boys were doing something they shouldn't be doing.

This first Proverb deals with this aspect of hiding what you are doing because your intentions are not proper. First, let us look at the positive side of this Proverb—**"Blessings are on the head of the righteous"** (10:6a). God blesses all people in certain aspects (Matthew 5:45; Psalm

145:9) but He abundantly blesses those who are godly. He showers them with blessings (Ezekiel 34:26; Luke 6:38) beyond what they can even handle. The godly are easily seen. Their good works from a sincere heart are in view for all to see—not from a standpoint of pride but as an example to those around as Jesus Himself commanded (Matthew 5:16), so those who see will glorify God.

"But the mouth of the wicked conceals violence" (10:6b). Those who do evil, hide their deeds. In John 3:19–20, Jesus said, **"This is the judgment, that the Light has come into the world, and men loved the darkness rather than the Light, for their deeds were evil. For everyone who does evil hates the Light, and does not come to the Light for fear that his deeds will be exposed."** Those who do evil do so in secret for as long as they can. We have all found ourselves in this predicament at one time or another, trying to hide our sin.

I read a survey several years ago concerning the habits of men who claimed to be Christians. I don't remember the exact numbers or where the survey came from, but it basically said that more than half (much more than half as I remember) of these Christian men regularly viewed pornography. These numbers were dramatically higher than years past because of the advent of the Internet. This dramatic rise was due to the fact that these Christian men could access pornography in complete secrecy—at least, secret from other people. They didn't have to walk into a convenience store to buy a magazine or go into the corner section of the video store—both of which are in the public's view.

I had a friend who was a pastor who was caught viewing pornography on the church computer. He left his church, left his wife, and left his children to find some woman he met on the Internet. He had been "secretly" indulging in his sin for over a year while pastoring his church.

As with many of the Proverbs, there is a choice. This choice is between living a godly life out in the open for all to see, or living an evil life that we must hide. Do not choose the way of the child who gets all too quiet when doing something he or she shouldn't be doing, or the way of the person Jesus says chooses the darkness rather than choosing Him.

If we must conceal anything about our lives, should we be trusted with riches of any kind, let alone the true riches that Jesus speaks of in Luke 16:11? **"Therefore if you have not been faithful in the use of unrighteous wealth, who will entrust the true riches to you?"** And what is at the core of even being tempted to do such things that must be hidden?

A popular song in the 1960s bemoaned the elusiveness of satisfaction. The song mentioned the influence of television commercials telling him that his shirts could be whiter, etc. We live in a world that is not satisfied with anything. We all want what we don't have.

Solomon has a cure for this disease in our next Proverb—**"The soul of the sluggard craves and gets nothing, but the soul of the diligent is made fat"** (13:4).

One characteristic of the sluggard is that he or she is never satisfied with their life or their possessions. They always want more stuff and they want it given to them. They don't want to put in the hard work to earn this stuff—they just want the stuff. A sluggard in our time could be the person who refuses to work or, at least, refuses to work hard enough to keep a decent job. A sluggard could be the teenager who doesn't apply himself or herself at school to better themselves and make themselves more marketable in the corporate world. They just want the high-paying job without obtaining the knowledge and the skills to warrant that pay. Lazy people, in this sense, want much but get nothing!

So, how do we reach contentment and satisfaction in our lives? Solomon says the cure is diligence or hard work. Satisfaction comes from a job well done. Satisfaction comes from putting in a full day—whether that is on the job, in the classroom, or at home. In another book that Solomon wrote, he says, **"Whatever your hand finds to do, do it with all your might; for there is no activity or planning or knowledge or wisdom in Sheol where you are going"** (Ecclesiastes 9:10). Now, Solomon wrote Ecclesiastes with a fatalist attitude, but the point is still valid—we must find something worthwhile to do with our lives and then do it well. Put your all into it. Don't waste your life in front of the television or playing video games for hours on end. Work hard on a worthy goal or pursuit.

It is easy in our culture to kick back and think that we deserve the good life, think things should be handed to us on a silver platter, but that is a lie of Satan. Nothing of any real value on this earth will ever just be handed to you. You can spend your life being lazy and always wanting more stuff, and then also look back and see a wasted mediocre life. Or you can work hard at obtaining knowledge and wisdom, and you can work hard at the job you have, and you can work hard at the ministry God has for your life. Then you can look back at a life well lived; you can look forward to hearing God say to you, "Well done, good and faithful servant."

Our satisfaction is in God and in following the principles He has left us in His Book. One of those principles is to work hard to be satisfied. If you truly want satisfaction and contentment, absorb God's Word and apply its principles to your life through the effort it requires.

Being satisfied can be a good thing but it can also be a bad thing. It is good to be satisfied, or content, with certain aspects of your life—like being content with living within your means instead of using credit to purchase unnecessary luxuries. It is bad to be satisfied, or content, with your current level of spiritual maturity; you should be seeking to grow in this regard through your entire lifetime.

This next Proverb simply makes a statement about this issue of satisfaction, but, in doing so, the implication is clear—**"Sheol and Abaddon are never satisfied, nor are the eyes of man ever satisfied"** (27:20).

Sheol and Abaddon are terms for death and the grave. Sheol and Abaddon are never satisfied, meaning people dying and being put into graves continues every minute of every day somewhere in the world; there is never a point where Sheol and Abaddon say, *"Okay, we've reached our limit; you can stop dying now, people."*

Solomon uses the fact of death and the grave never being satisfied to drive home his main point—man's desire for things is also never satisfied. The appetite of our eyes is voracious and unending. We are bombarded with advertisements in the paper, on television, in our email, on billboards, in storefront windows, etc. We pour fuel on the fire by giving attention to these ads; stoking our desire to own and possess; feeding the sin of covetousness.

The comparison of human greed with the ruthless, unsparing, and destructive realm of death suggests that its craving is also ruthless, destructive, and insatiable. The unending appetite to desire more and better and newer leads to lusting after each other's homes, spouses, and property. It is an ugly downward spiral if not intentionally held in check.

But we must be careful to make sure we apply this truth to all areas of our lives, otherwise we could be in danger of applying this truth to other people and not ourselves. It's easy to look at the millionaire and deride the fact that they own twenty-five cars and how much of a waste that is but overlook the humungous collections of movies and music you have that are still being added to, or the closet full of clothes, or the … **nor are the eyes of man ever satisfied**.

Curb your appetite. Take a good look at your purchasing habits. If you aren't sure if you are out of control, try going six months without purchasing any items that aren't fulfilling your basic needs (not wants). If you find it difficult, then you can rest assured there is at least some measure of a problem in that area. Discipline yourself to be satisfied and content.

* * *

As I sit at my desk typing, on the bookshelf to my left are fifteen different Bibles. Another one is open to the Book of Proverbs on my desk in front of me, and the computer program I use in my studies has a parallel Bible opened with fourteen different translations tiled on my screen. My guess is that I have at least that many copies of the Scripture on the bookshelves of my church office. Some of these volumes have probably not been cracked open for years if not a decade or more; others are well-worn and tattered. I would guess that, while most of you have nowhere near that tally of Bibles in your possession, you probably have more than one or two at your disposal.

I have heard stories from missionaries who have been in countries where it is illegal to own a Bible. The Christians in these countries sometimes have a page or a scrap of a page from God's Word and they cherish and treasure it above all their other earthly possessions. I have to wonder how we compare in how much we value the multiple volumes of God's Word we possess.

This next Proverb speaks to this difference in attitude—**"A sated man loathes honey, but to a famished man any bitter thing is sweet"** (27:7).

The word sated means satisfied or full in the sense of their appetite, with a sense of actually being too full. Most of us could say we are sated after Thanksgiving or Christmas dinner when you reach the point of not being able to stuff another fork full in your mouth. A sated person doesn't even want to look at or smell food for a while. On the other hand, someone who is famished is not picky about what foods are given to them. In the sense of this Proverb, we are talking about someone who is destitute and is happy to have anything edible to eat; even celery is sweet to his or her palate.

There are many applications for this Proverb, the primary of which is to be thankful for what you have and to never take for granted the provision of God. But since we are attempting to grow in our understanding of handling money, how's your appetite for God's wisdom? Have you been sated with the glut of entertainment options that there is precious little room for God's wisdom? Are you so stuffed with social media posts that you can't fit in a word from God?

It's a sobering thought. We are so blessed in this country. Take advantage of this blessing and develop a healthy hunger and thirst for the things of God.

Along the same lines, Mom loved to cook. She prepared feasts for fifteen to twenty people even when only eight were coming to dinner. Family dinners would include two main courses, macaroni and cheese, corn on the cob complete with the melted butter dribbling down your chin, double baked potatoes, green beans, sweet potatoes (and I mean sweet), etc. Desserts of German chocolate cake, coconut cake, peach cobbler, cheesecake, peanut butter fudge, etc., were strewn across the counter. I'm sure Mom is consulting with God concerning the marriage supper of the Lamb right now.

Mom also loved picky eaters. She would prepare certain dishes, especially for each child or grandchild at the table. I was one of those picky eaters. As a young boy, I did not like the taste or the texture of ricotta cheese in my lasagna. No problem—Mom simply made a small pan of lasagna with only mozzarella cheese just for me. The grandchildren loved macaroni and cheese, so macaroni and cheese was prepared at every family dinner. The sin of gluttony was not mentioned at Mom's house.

The next Proverb is not about overeating, but again about satisfaction and contentment—**"The righteous has enough to satisfy his appetite, but the stomach of the wicked is in need"** (13:25).

Contentment, as we should be discovering, is elusive for most of us. What may bring contentment today may not do so tomorrow. Sticking with the illustration of food, I enjoy a good pizza (and moving from Chicago to Colorado means I don't get to enjoy a good pizza very often) but I can only handle eating even a good pizza for so many days in a row. I will eventually grow discontented with pizza for dinner. The same goes for my Christian life if I am not careful. I may be content with the lot in life God has for me today but grow weary of my situation tomorrow.

Through the first forty or so years of my life, I dealt with financial struggles (many, by my own admission, were self-inflicted). God helped me grow to where I am content with whatever level of financial prosperity I possess—He has shown me that He will provide as the need arises (**"Give us this day our daily bread"** NOT *"Give us this day our bread for the whole year"*). If I am not careful, I could look upon the lot in life God has given others and become discontented with my lot.

Solomon tells us that our contentment is inseparably connected to our godliness. The more righteousness and godliness we pour into our lives, the more contented we will be with whatever comes our way.

The Apostle Paul had this type of godly contentment—**"Not that I speak from want, for I have learned to be content in whatever** circumstances I am. I know how to get along with humble means, and I also know how to live in prosperity; in any and every circumstance I have learned the secret of being filled and going hungry, both of having abundance and suffering need. I can do all things through Him who strengthens me" (Philippians 4:11–13). And notice the context of the oft quoted verse 13—"I can do all things through Him who strengthens me," once I finally learned contentment.

On the other side of the equation are the ungodly or the wicked—they are never content and never will be.

As a Christian, we can use this as another barometer to see how closely we are walking with God. Are you content with your lot in life? If so, you are probably on the right track. If not, ask God to reveal any issues in that your life are causing discontent. For the Christian, the only times you could rightly be in discontent would be concerning your own personal spiritual growth—and, even then, we need to be patient with God. Some things cannot be learned overnight or without the necessary experience.

So, feast upon God's Word today and every day until your heart learns contentment. The more you feast, the more content you will become with all things. And, as contentment germinates, your outlook and attitude will be where it should be.

Generally speaking then, what is your attitude on a day-to-day basis? When you wake up in the morning are your first thoughts—*Wow! Another day to live and enjoy. What a blessing!* Or, are your first thoughts—*I wish I didn't have to work today. I really hate having to work.* Or, are your first thoughts—*Coffee!* Besides the thought of getting that first cup of coffee, most of us probably fall somewhere in between the first two extremes. An even greater majority of people probably does not consider that their attitude on any given day matters much—but it does.

Solomon points this out in this next Proverb—**"All the days of the afflicted are bad, but a cheerful heart has a continual feast"** (15:15).

If, in general, you have a poor attitude about anything, you are causing self-inflicted pain. Your attitude indeed makes a major difference in your life. We have all probably heard the expression, *"If you think you can or you think you can't, you're right!"* And while that expression may not always be completely accurate, your attitude will most definitely have an effect on the outcome of any particular situation.

Let's say you are on a gurney being wheeled into the operating room. Would you want the surgeon who is wringing his hands and mumbling to himself, *"I don't know about this one, this is bad"*? Or would you want the surgeon who is upbeat and saying, *"You know I haven't had to deal with an operation quite like this one before, but I am extremely confident that everything will turn out wonderful when all is said and done"*? Both surgeons may have the same level of skill and training, and both may have the same impeccable record of never losing a patient, but, if you had the choice, which one would you want operating on you?

Understand that having a positive attitude will not allow you to do anything you want. For example, at the time of this writing I could stand to lose some weight. I could have the best attitude ever recorded in the annals of history and I would still be a horrible jockey in a horse race. I also could not dunk a basketball and I could not run a marathon no matter how good my attitude was. But a good attitude will help me do everything better than if I had a poor attitude.

Solomon says, for those who do have a good attitude, life is a continual feast. Life is a continuing series of choices just like walking through the line of a smorgasbord. No matter what happens to you, you have the choice of how you are going to respond. You can choose to be negative, throw up your hands and cry, *"Why me?"* Or, you can choose to be positive and look to the Lord for the good that He has planned for you even through difficult circumstances. Every day can bring trouble, or every day can be a feast. The choice is quite frankly up to you.

The Bible commands us to rejoice always and to give thanks always. When we allow our circumstances to dictate our attitude or emotions for the day, we are revealing our lack of trust in the Lord. So, put a smile on your face and praise the Lord! He knows what you are facing today, and He is right there with you to help you grow through it.

Yet, few have been able to slay the beast of materialism; few even desire such. Most of us want bigger and better and more, and we will sacrifice our futures to have it. Billions of dollars are spent every year on advertising that is designed to keep you in a state of discontent—and it's working!

For many years, I would have gone toe-to-toe with anyone who called me materialistic, but God opened my eyes to the truth not too many years ago. My want of things and stuff had, to some extent, consumed my life. I was duped into making poor choices with credit. I believed the lies of Satan instead of believing what God says in His Word.

Even though my past life is not worthy of writing this book, God has lovingly corrected me and brought this work to fruition. I am still learning with you on how to completely apply the principles God has given us, but it continues to be a struggle at times.

A man named Agur (who takes over for Solomon in these last two Proverbs on attitude and contentment) understood this struggle all too well—**"Two things I asked of You, do not refuse me before I die: Keep deception and lies far from me, give me neither poverty nor riches; feed me with the food that is my portion, that I not be full and deny You and say, 'Who is the Lord?' Or that I not be in want and steal, and profane the name of my God"** (30:7–9).

God has blessed America immensely during our respectively brief existence. He has done so primarily because we have, by and large, trusted in Him from the beginning. That trust in God has severely waned through the years; there really is only a remnant that remains. Our churches are abandoning the Bible almost as fast as our government has. Some never even turn to the Word of God during their "sermons," making it hard to know why it is even called a sermon anymore.

I know I am getting a little off track, but the point I am getting to is that we have abused the blessings of God. And when I say "we," I am speaking to genuine believers. Believers are responsible for keeping God first in our lives and in our country. We are the ones who have stood idly by and allowed God to be pushed out of every institution of our land. We cannot expect the unbelievers to practice God's righteousness; that's not only foolish, it is not biblical.

God's Word says the ones "**who are called by My name humble themselves and pray and seek My face and turn from their wicked ways, then I will hear from heaven, will forgive their sin and will heal their land**" (2 Chronicles 7:14). God isn't waiting for unbelievers to turn from their wicked ways, He is waiting for His people to do so.

And one connection I wish to make here that pertains to our study in this book—a "wicked way" is debt! God warns us again and again in His Word to avoid debt. He tells us we are willingly enslaving ourselves when we use credit, yet we do so and have done so day after day.

There is hope, though, as there always is with our awesome God, and it falls in line with our continuing look at contentment.

Discontented people combined with easy access to money or credit, or combined with no access to money or credit, is a recipe for disaster either way.

A child who is not bombarded by all of the television ads is thrilled with any gift he or she receives on Christmas morning. A child who sat in front of the television during the entire holiday season is disappointed they didn't get everything. And that discontent and disappointment is not limited to children.

Our Proverb shows us that there is danger in poverty as well as riches if we are discontent, because discontentment in your situation and circumstances is actually discontentment in God. We always need someone to blame for our condition and it will eventually get around to God, which will ultimately manifest itself into sin against God.

Genuine contentment comes from an understanding that this life is just a blip on the radar of eternity. Make the most of your time here. Be diligent in the vocation you have, be content to live within your means, avoid debt like the plague, and, in due time, you will prosper and you will minimize the danger of denying God or profaning His name.

But our new friend, Agur, is not done.

Of all the worries you could amass on a daily basis, they all fall into two categories: issues you have absolutely no control over and issues you have some measure of control over. For the ones you have some measure of control over, get busy and do what you can to alleviate the problem; for the ones you have absolutely no control over, turn them over to God and put them out of your mind. But most people prefer to just keep worrying, allowing these worries to suck the joy right out of their lives.

Agur opens this next Proverb with a vivid, if not somewhat disgusting illustration—**"The leech has two daughters, 'Give,' 'Give'"** (30:15a).

A leech is a nasty creature that tends to proliferate in stagnant waters. In ancient Israel, they were common and are usually called horse leeches because of their tendency to attach themselves inside the nostrils and on the palates of horses when they drank from these waters. Horse leeches were so common that the Talmud even warns of drinking water from ponds by mouth. But while leeches will literally eat themselves to death and can cause physical problems to people and animals, you can avoid or eliminate them from your life; you have a great measure of control over the dangers that leeches impose.

Agur goes on to mention four things that also are never satisfied, but we have no control over these—**"There are three things that will not be satisfied, four that will not say, 'Enough': Sheol, and the barren womb, earth that is never satisfied with water, and fire that never says, 'Enough'"** (30:15b–16).

Death (Sheol) never gets its fill (as we studied a bit earlier); there isn't a quota that is, at some point, reached where death says, **"Enough."** A barren womb is never satisfied; time may march on, but the passing of time does not bring complete satisfaction. The ground above sea level is never fully satisfied; even after an unusually wet spring, there will come a point during the summer when the ground will crack, crying out for more water. And finally, a raging fire doesn't consume only a certain number of trees if left unchecked; as long as there is more to consume, the fire will continue to do so.

Our worries in this life fall into these two categories. We cannot stop death, we cannot satisfy an empty womb, we cannot water our gardens and be done with it forever, and, although we can stop an individual fire, we cannot stop fire from ever happening again. These fall into the category of worries we must turn over to God and leave them in His capable hands. Trying to control the uncontrollable is like trying to eliminate a headache while banging your head against a wall.

We can avoid and eliminate the leeches that come into our lives. These kinds of worries are also never satisfied if you allow them into your life and choose to not do anything about them, but you can do something about them!

Allow me to offer this one application in closing this brief look into Agur's wisdom: Regardless of which kind of worries you face, the remedy for dealing with any of them is genuinely believing the promises of God. This is what you have control over and what you can do about the leeches of worry in your life. You have control over how often you open your Bible. You have control over how deeply you study. You have control over how much of God's Word you believe and apply. And thus, you have control over the joy that is active in your life.

On Being Generous

I enjoy sports. I am beyond being able to enjoy participating much anymore but I can still watch them on TV with the best. Baseball is my favorite, but ever since I coached my son's football team many years ago, I have become more enthralled with the teamwork aspect of this game. I find myself watching all of the "secondary" action in a football game instead of simply watching the player who has the ball. In football, all eleven players have a job to do on every play, even if the ball is not going to be anywhere near them. If an offensive guard fails to block the defensive lineman, it doesn't matter how good your quarterback is—he is going to get hammered. If the wide receiver does not do a good job of convincing the defense that the ball is coming his way (even when it is not), the defense can quickly adjust and stop who is really getting the ball. There are so many intricacies to the game. Even when it seems like only one or two players are the main stars, without the other nine or ten players, they would fail. It takes a coordinated effort of teamwork to win.

This next nugget of wisdom from Solomon deals with teamwork—and the team is Christianity. All of us who have confessed Jesus Christ as Lord are on the same team. And all of us have a specific job to do for this team to be successful. One aspect of teamwork is helping someone who has fallen down when you have the ability to help.

Solomon says, "**Do not withhold good from those to whom it is due, when it is in your power to do it**" (3:27). In a football game, there are many times when one of the players fails in his attempt to do his job. A good teammate, who has the chance to help, will step in and do the job for his fallen comrade—and thus help the entire team accomplish their goal.

In Christianity we must be on the alert for those who have fallen and those who are struggling to get the job done—those who are being defeated by the enemy. When we have the ability to help, we must step in and help.

The Apostle John has this to say about Christian teamwork in 1 John 3:17, "**But whoever has the world's goods, and sees his brother in need and closes his heart against him, how does the love of God abide in him?**" In 2 Corinthians 8:14–15, the Apostle Paul has this to say regarding Christian teamwork, "**At this present time your abundance being a supply for their need, so that their abundance also may become *a supply* for your need that there may be equality; as it is written, 'He who *gathered* much did not have too much, and he who *gathered* little had no lack.'**"

And we must not wait when opportunities to help are before us. If you can help your neighbor now, "**Do not say to your neighbor, 'Go, and come back, and tomorrow I will give it' when you have it with you.**" (3:28). When God gives you an opportunity to help, your duty is to jump in at that very moment and help. I learned this lesson the hard way. One time in my life (and almost only one time), I had a hundred-dollar bill in my pocket. At church, one evening, I felt the Lord prompting me to give that hundred-dollar bill to another member of our church who was going through some tough times. I didn't. I felt horrible later that night and vowed to give that money away the next time I saw the person. But, the next time I saw him, I no longer had a hundred dollars to give—the opportunity to do good had passed. I let down my team that day.

The examples I have used dealt with money, but the principle goes so much farther. We can help our teammates by encouraging them when they are down, by teaching them when they are lacking in knowledge, by hugging them when they are lonely, by loving them at all times, etc.

God is in control of all things and He will supply your needs when you obey His Word in helping others when the need is before you, which is the lesson in this next Proverb.

In the 1985 comedy, *Brewster's Millions*, Richard Pryor plays the character of Montgomery Brewster. Monty's rich uncle dies at the opening of the film and leaves Monty with an inheritance of $300 million dollars—but there is a catch. Monty must spend $30 million in thirty days and not have any assets to show for that $30 million—meaning that he couldn't buy a car or a house or clothes or anything else that he would still possess at the end of the thirty days. He also could not tell anyone about the deal and was limited in the amount he could just give away to charities and other people.

This is not the greatest analogy of our current Proverb, but it is in some ways how God views the money He allows us to have. It is not to be spent only on our wants and our desires, or to accumulate earthly possessions. God wants us to be channels, or streams, that receive from Him and then distribute to those who have need. Sadly, most who call themselves Christians are ponds and lakes who receive from God and accumulate in their own backyards. Our society and culture promote this attitude of hoarding.

Solomon says, **"There is one who scatters, and *yet* increases all the more"** (11:24a). This law of God is confirmed in other passages of Scripture (2 Corinthians 9:6–7; Luke 6:38). The more freely you give what God has blessed you with, the more freely God will resupply, and then some.

On the flip side, Solomon says, **"and there is one who withholds what is justly due, *and yet it results* only in want"** (11:24b). Even if you manage to die a wealthy person, none of that wealth is going with you. But even while still on this earth, those who hoard everything and never generously give to others are miserable people inside. Their miserliness eats away at them as they become obsessed with protecting and accumulating more. They are never content and satisfied but are paranoid that everyone they meet is only after their money.

The final principle in this Proverb deals with one of the earthly benefits of living generously—**"The generous man will be prosperous, and he who waters will himself be watered"** (11:25). God is watching how each of us handles the wealth He gives to us. God watches to see how we use this wealth, and He, in turn, blesses those who are generous with more wealth.

We are stewards, or managers, of the money we receive—not owners. How we handle this responsibility in large part determines if God will allow us to be responsible for even greater riches (material and otherwise).

While you do not have the charge to be wasteful as Monty Brewster had, you do have the charge to be generous with what you have been given. As you are faithful in carrying out this charge, God may then provide you with more to be generous with.

I have one last Proverb in this chapter on the topic of generosity, but with a different slant.

When couples come to me asking if I would officiate their wedding ceremony, or when I simply attend a wedding, or when a couple comes to me in need of marriage counseling, and, quite often, in the course of preaching a sermon, I ask the question, *"What is the opposite of love?"* Almost invariably the response is *"Hate."* At that point I explain that the proper answer is actually selfishness. Because genuine love will always do what is best for the other person as opposed to doing what is best for themselves if a choice has to be made.

Based upon this definition, it is easy to determine that there is precious little genuine love in this world, because most everyone is infinitely more interested in themselves than in other people. We are so wrapped up in our own little worlds that we either ignore or have become so conditioned and hardened to the plight of other people around us.

Once when my wife and I traveled 1,200 miles to visit with family and friends over Christmas, a person we desired to spend some time with could not find it within themselves to rearrange their daily routine over the course of that week to even have lunch with us before we headed back home. There weren't any issues of past offences or hard feelings, they simply chose to not be inconvenienced.

This is the underlying premise of this final Proverb in this chapter—**"The righteous is concerned for the rights of the poor, the wicked does not understand *such* concern"** (29:7).

The mantra being taught, emphasized, and repeated over the last several decades at least, is to look out for number one. We are bombarded with the promotion of self-worth, self-esteem, self-fulfillment, and self-love. We are conditioned to always ask, "*What's in it for me?*" The constant complaint in marriages-gone-bad is, "*My needs aren't being fulfilled.*" It truly is the Me Generation.

Solomon is telling us that the righteous are people who express genuine biblical love for others. The righteous are selfless not selfish. The righteous are always looking out for those who may have a need as opposed to looking out for number one—which, by the way, the phrase "*Looking out for number one*" is actually a very good one as long as we understand that God is number One. With that understanding, we will be earnestly striving to be obedient to His Word, and thus be living a life of righteous choices, which means we will exude a genuine care, compassion, and love for others.

This love for others obviously extends to the poor—the main application of our Proverb today. Having a genuine concern for those who are in need proves you are on the right path. Having no concern for the poor proves you to be wicked, according to this Proverb.

So, again, what's the opposite of love?

This was primarily the attitudes we must employ to activate what we are studying about financial wisdom. In part 2, we will address some specific activities we must incorporate.

* * *

TAKE ACTION

Personal attitudes are often very difficult to adjust, but they must be checked and dealt with regularly. I was raised in a loving Christian home, yet I must fight almost on a daily basis to keep my attitude where it must be. There is no apparent reason for my internal battle with negative thoughts, but they are there.

For me, I must feed my mind with positive motivational books and lectures, the Scripture, sermons, and uplifting music. I must avoid the radio talk shows, the TV news, and the unending drama on social media like the plague. To keep my attitude where it needs to be, I am keenly aware of what I read, listen to, watch, and who I spend the most time with.

Take stock of what you allow into your mind. What are your daily habits? Do you start and end your day with the overtly negative TV news? Do you listen to talk radio that likely elevates your blood pressure on the way to and from work? What do the television programs you watch on a nightly basis do for you? Are they helping your attitude or hurting it? Advertising is expertly crafted and designed to make you discontent, so you will be motivated to make a purchase—how many of them are you reading and listening to and watching each day?

You can take steps to limit the impact all of the negative input and increase the positive input. Figure out what needs to change for you and do it now!

CHAPTER 11

MISS THESE AND YOU HAVE
MISSED EVERYTHING (PART 2)

L et's dive right into this final chapter on a few essentials that we simply must not miss. I touched on several of the attitudes that need to be internalized in the last chapter; in this chapter, we must take hold of several actions or activities that need to become part of our identity as genuine believers. We are known by our fruit, and these final words from Solomon will reveal if that fruit is genuine in our worthy pursuit of handling our finances as God has designed.

On Handling Money

How prepared are you? Most of you probably just had the question come to mind, "*Prepared for what, Al?*" And therein lies the point that needs to be made today—being prepared for the unexpected.

Solomon speaks of the folly of not being prepared—**"An inheritance gained hurriedly at the beginning will not be blessed in the end"** (20:21). Specifically, Solomon is speaking of not being prepared to handle unexpected money. And while all of you now have visions dancing in your head of inheriting a wad of cash, most of us are not prepared to deal with quick riches in a biblical manner. So, let's look at the specifics of this Proverb and then try to make application to all areas of our lives—not just handling unexpected wealth.

Money has tremendous power over people. It does not matter if you currently have much or have little. You can be a Christian or a pagan and fall under the same spell. The allurement of riches affects people of every race, creed, or color. You can be tall or short, skinny or fat, smart or ignorant, and still stumble into the same traps when it comes to handling wealth. The desire for money causes marriages to crumble, corporations to fail, and nations to go to war. People will kill for money and commit many other despicable acts against themselves and against humanity. Yes indeed, money has tremendous power over people.

The Hebrew word translated as "**at the beginning**" is not necessarily referring to receiving an inheritance at a young age. The usage of the word varies, and there are many subtle nuances, but there is no clear indication of it being used in an age-related manner. It is more commonly translated in the sense of a hasty beginning or a sudden change of circumstances. There is a sense of inexperience playing a major role in the misuse of riches. Solomon's point lies in not being properly prepared, and thus seeing ruin come to your life instead of blessing.

Lessons are hard when you are not looking for one. As I alluded to much earlier, I blindly invested in the futures market and gained more money in a few weeks than I had ever earned in a year prior to that. I was not ready for the instant windfall. What could have been a tremendous blessing ended in ruin as I quickly lost all my gains. I simply was not prepared to handle that kind of money that quickly.

But we can take this application beyond properly handling unexpected riches. So, how do we prepare for the unexpected in any area of life, including money? The premise of the entire Book of Proverbs gives us the answer: Seek and acquire God's wisdom with every fiber of your being. Fill you mind and fill your heart with God's wisdom by reading, studying, memorizing, meditating upon, and applying the Scripture every day, or—as my congregation hears from me often—daily, deeply, and desperately. In doing so, you will have absolutely everything you need to handle anything that comes your way (2 Peter 1:3).

I trust you have been picking up at least a few helpful nuggets of wisdom in handling money and possessions. I also trust this Proverb has helped you see the importance of being prepared for the blessings to come as you adhere to Solomon's wisdom on the subject.

* * *

We know that money is a neutral commodity. There is nothing inherently good nor inherently evil about money. When I was a child, I won ten dollars from a Sunday school contest at church. When going home in the car that afternoon, my younger brother (obviously either wanting the money for himself or not wanting me to have it) misquoted 1 Timothy 6:10 by saying, *"Money is the root of all evil."* That verse is still misquoted in this same way today. The verse actually says, "**For the love of money is a root of all sorts of evil, and some by longing for it have wandered away from the faith and pierced themselves with many griefs**." There are great dangers in loving money, but money in and of itself is not evil—it is simply a neutral commodity.

This next Proverb deals with how different people use the money they have and continues to teach us valuable lessons.

The first person we meet is a godly person—"**The wages of the righteous is life**" (10:16a). A godly person understands the proper use of money. She also understands the proper attitude she must have toward money. And, because of this, her earnings enhance her life—it doesn't rule her life.

Money is necessary for our existence in the culture and economy we live in, but most Americans (even Christians) have turned it into a god to be worshipped. We spend the better part of everyday thinking about and pursuing money. We misuse credit by buying bigger houses than we need, and nicer cars than are necessary, and big screen televisions, etc., to the point of absolutely requiring more money just to keep up with our minimum monthly payments. Our one consuming thought each day then becomes money. Our earnings no longer enhance our lives, the pursuit of earnings consumes our lives.

This is not God's design, which is why He speaks about money and its use throughout the Bible more than any other single topic—more than heaven, more than hell, even more than salvation. We must keep a careful eye on how we use the money God gives us. If necessary, we must scale back and be content with our position in life instead of trying to keep up with our friends, family, and neighbors. We must get to where our earnings enhance our lives instead of being consumed with the pursuit of more.

The second person we meet is the evil person—**"the income of the wicked, punishment"** (10:16b). The evil person pursues money and worships money and is consumed with thoughts of money in the same way a Christian can be at times, but the difference is in how he spends his money. The amount of money spent on sinful things and sinful desires is staggering. By far the most profitable venture on the Internet is and always has been the pornography industry. Not too long ago, it was estimated that more than 50% of all profits made on the Internet came from pornography. This is the point Solomon is making on the abuse of money.

Again, money is a neutral commodity. What we do with money and how we view money has tremendous implications on our lives. Do whatever is necessary to align yourself with God's purpose and plan for how you should be viewing and using the money in which He entrusts to your care. We must be careful to avoid being people who neglect the proper use of money.

One way we accomplish using and viewing money in a biblical manner is simply to pay attention to the details and to end game, if you will. We must always inspect our motives and activities, and we cannot skip any of what God has to say on the subject.

"*When* the grass disappears, the new growth is seen, and the herbs of the mountains are gathered in, the lambs *will be* for your clothing, and the goats *will bring* the price of a field, and *there will be* goats'

milk enough for your food, for the food of your household, and sustenance for your maidens" (27:25–27).

If memory serves me correctly (which is really a shot in the dark most of the time), the Apollo 13 explosion in outer space that almost cost the lives of three astronauts was caused by a faulty O-Ring in an auxiliary oxygen tank; a very inexpensive and seemingly insignificant part in respect to the millions spent on the entire spacecraft. Whether this defect could have been detected beforehand is not known, but you better believe that quality control and detailed inspections of subsequent missions increased exponentially. Apollo 13 was not the last disaster for NASA, but it once again emphasized the importance of following a detailed process before sending a crew up in space. When everything is done perfectly and in order, the chances for success increase accordingly.

The Proverb listed above (27:25–27) may seem like a list of random observations by someone out in the fields, but it is actually showing us a progression of what happens in your life if you heed the advice of the 27:23–24, which we looked at in chapter 8—"**Know well the condition of your flocks, *and* pay attention to your herds; for riches are not forever, nor does a crown *endure* to all generations.**"

In other words, if you pay attention to and follow the process God has given to you, the results will be provision and prosperity. The **new growth** is the feed for the livestock. The **herbs** also denote the wild food for grazing. As the flocks and herds are well-fed, they produce wool for **clothing** and money when you sell a portion of your livestock. The animals also provide **food** and **sustenance** for you, your **household**, and many others.

If a careless herdsman did not pay attention to the flocks and herds, they could wander off into dangerous places, fall into ravines, be attacked by wild animals, or stolen by thieves; they could even end up in areas where the vegetation is poisonous. Without the proper care of the flocks and herds, the entire cycle of provision and prosperity is derailed.

We have a great tendency to skip many steps in God's process for provision and prosperity. We somehow believe that we know better than

God. We think we are the exception to the rule and can get away with shortcutting the biblical process. For example, God may warn us about the many dangers of debt, but we deceive ourselves and believe we can handle it; the warnings are for other people, not us. But, ultimately, we are overlooking the faulty O-Rings in our lives. We are a disaster waiting to happen by ignoring one or more steps in God's procedure.

As I mentioned much earlier, I have been guilty of this type of arrogance for far too many years. In times past, I have skipped over many steps in God's procedure, thinking that my obedience in other areas will cover over any lack in this one. It doesn't work that way. Make sure you know God's processes by being a student of His Word, and then make sure you follow the procedure so you will reap the benefits—the provision and prosperity.

The struggle we often face in following God's principles is they do not always match our human logic or personal inclinations.

The Bible is clear that we are to be good stewards of the money God entrusts to our care; and this applies to individuals as well as churches. Biblical stewardship, though, many times deals more with how the money is being used more so than the amount being used. I once attempted to make a point in a sermon to a situation we faced at our church that connects with this next Proverb.

At the time, my church was almost four years old. From day one, God supplied our every financial need. Even though we were a small mountain church, we fasted, prayed, and trusted God to provide us with a piece of property and the funds to build a church without incurring debt of any kind. God honored our times of fasting and prayer and trust in Him to the tune of having thirty-nine acres of land donated to us, along with $500,000 to build with.

Before this miraculous provision, we began to tighten up our spending as our offerings versus expenses was narrowing. It wasn't that we were overly frivolous, and we were not in immediate danger of not being able to pay our bills on time, but there were some areas that needed attention. The church had purchased a used vehicle for my use that used up the surplus funds we had in our general account. We did a little more belt-tightening and then began operating week to week. We found ourselves relying on the current week's offerings to pay for the previous week's expenditures.

The question in my mind was: Is it a coincidence that, at the point we tightened up our spending, the church finances started becoming a concern? Since I do not believe in coincidences, I couldn't help but wonder if, somehow, our self-imposed belt tightening was in some small way exhibiting a lack of faith. Did we start looking at our church finances from a man-centered point of view instead of from God's point of view? God doesn't operate according to the state of the economy or any other human realm; He operates according to the truth that He owns all the silver and all the gold and the cattle on a thousand hills.

"A faithful man will abound with blessings" (28:20a), meaning, those who operate their lives exclusively by faith and not by sight will never experience lack. But lest we are tempted to have an improper attitude concerning this truth, our Proverb goes on to say, **"but he who makes haste to be rich will not go unpunished"** (28:20b), meaning, those who have visions of being wealthy and focus their attention on this pursuit will be punished for this attitude. And it is not a stretch of the imagination to say the punishment is lack. **"There is one who scatters, and *yet* increases all the more, and there is one who withholds what is justly due, *and yet it results* only in want"** (11:24).

The pursuit of riches almost always includes a measure of hoarding that which is obtained. Accumulation is the name of the game when you are trying to gain wealth. God's plan is to not to accumulate but to circulate. We should never be ponds that only receive water, we are to be streams that receive and then send out. At any point in the process, we control the flow. When we restrict putting God's money to proper use, God restricts the flow to us. When we generously and properly disburse what God gives us, He increases the flow. God responds to our actions, which actually means God responds to our measure of faith.

Once we regained our focus as a church to follow God's leading instead of being focused on the state of our finances, God supplied. Faith won. It was not too long after this learning experience that the miracles came fast. We not only were given the land and the funds to build and furnish, we were able to expand our original building a few years later (also debt-free), and my salary was increased, so I could sell my insurance business and devote all my time to the ministry of the church.

It's amazing, although we should not be surprised, what God does when we trust in Him and follow His design; but it is only as we trust, honor, revere, and fear Him and His Word.

My wife and I enjoy taking vacations, as I am sure most of you do. We do not get the opportunity to do so very often (most of our time off has been to visit family over the past decade or so), but when we do get the chance and can afford it, we thoroughly enjoy seeing new places and relaxing for a week or so.

In the early years of our marriage, by God's blessing and provision, we had the chance to visit Oahu in the Hawaiian Islands. Each day we got up, had breakfast, and then traveled around every corner of the island we could reach by car. Each night, we would return to Honolulu, have dinner, walk the beach or the shopping district, and relax. It was the trip of a lifetime for us.

While we could have suffered through that pace of life for another week or so, and although we were returning to cold Chicago, there was still something about getting back home.

Several years later, my wife was on a business trip in Toronto, Canada the day of the terrorist attacks on 9/11. Home for us was in the Denver area at the time, even though we had only lived there for less than a year. God provided her one of the last available rental cars and got across the border before they were closed down. Our son and I met her in Chicago and then drove home. Disaster had struck and our first instincts were to get the family together and get home.

The same kind of security and comfort that being home brings us, in some small way, is magnified to infinite proportions for those who know God; those who have confessed Jesus Christ as their Lord. Our present homes only offer us the feeling of safety and security. True safety and security only come from One source—**"In the fear of the LORD there is strong confidence, and his children will have refuge"** (14:26). Notice that safety and security are not a place, but a Person. God is that Person.

In the human realm, the life we live is the very definition of uncertainty. You can have excellent health one day and be in the hospital the next. You can be enjoying the fruits of a stable career on Tuesday and be filing for unemployment assistance on Wednesday. You can be riding on a spiritual high when you go to sleep at night and wake up to demonic attack and personal persecution the next morning. And, vice versa, all these incidents can be reversed; you can have poor health one day and good health the next, etc. If you hate change, then you might as well say you hate life because life is change.

But in the midst of all this turmoil and change going on around us and within us, we have available to us the security and refuge that is God. God is in complete control of all things; all things in this world and all things in your life. He never sleeps and He is never surprised by anything. Nothing ever happens in this universe that causes God to say, *"Uh oh! I didn't see that one coming!"* God sees all and already knows all that is coming. Not only that, but nothing happens without His allowance. Even the disasters of the world, whether man-made or natural, only happen if He allows them to happen (and I know that brings up a whole bunch of questions but that is not the focus of this book).

Those who fear the Lord are not only doing themselves a favor, but they are also providing the security and refuge to their children if they are so inclined to follow in their parent's footsteps. The children can always run Home as well. Home is where the heart is, so the saying goes. If we have given our hearts to the Lord, that saying is ever so true.

In the context of this book, you will never have true success with your finances apart from an undying trust in our Lord. Such trust must be active in any circumstance, any situation, and at any time. Worry and trust cannot coexist. Taking matters into your own hands and trust cannot coexist. Honoring God and His Word in all things is the only path.

On Giving

Let's do some arithmetic. Sharpen your pencils and break out your calculators—I have a test for you. Give me the answer to the following problems:

$$10 - 0 = ?$$
$$10 - 2 = ?$$
$$10 - 5 = ?$$

Okay, if you passed first grade math, you got the answers of 10, 8, and 5 (if you didn't, we need to talk). Now, tell me which of these numbers is the greatest—10, 8, or 5? The answer is 10 (very good class). This is the world's mathematics.

Now, let's look at God's mathematics. God's mathematics says (10 - 2) or (10 - 5) or (10 - anything) is greater than (10 - 0). In God's mathematics, the more you take away, the more you have. The first Proverb we will look at on giving says, **"Honor the LORD from your wealth and from the first of all your produce. So your barns will be filled with plenty and your vats will overflow with new wine"** (3:9–10). God does addition by subtraction. As we give to the Lord, He, in turn, gives back to us in greater and more abundant ways than we can imagine.

I'll have a brief word on the tithe in a moment, but God gives us the same principle of receiving as much or more than you give in return through His prophet, Malachi—**"'Bring the whole tithe into the storehouse, so that there may be food in My house, and test Me now in this,' says the LORD of hosts, 'if I will not open for you the windows of heaven and pour out for you a blessing until it overflows'"** (Malachi 3:10).

Jesus says in Luke 6:38, **"Give, and it will be given to you. They will pour into your lap a good measure—pressed down, shaken together, *and* running over. For by your standard of measure it will be measured to you in return."**

So, we may ask the question, *"How much do I give to honor the Lord?"* There is no simple mandated answer to that question in the Bible.

I trust I will not offend anyone with the following, but the original intent of the tithe was for the operation of the nation of Israel during the days of the Tabernacle/Temple while under the Old Covenant. And, if you insist that the tithe is still mandated for the church today, please note that Israel had three separate tithes—two were annual and a third was every three years.

Each tithe for Israel had a specific aspect of their national life to be funded. This is a very simplistic and insufficient explanation, but one of the annual tithes supported the upkeep of the Tabernacle/Temple and "paid" the priests and Levites for their service. If you wanted to force things, I guess you could try to correlate this to the church and paid staff members, but there are a lot of other issues you would need to force as well—including the pastor and staff not being able to own any personal land or have an additional job.

The second tithe funded the feasts and festivals (most of which were annual) that were mandated for the nation to observe. The third tithe (every three years) was Israel's welfare system for the needy and destitute. There were various other mandated offerings and then several voluntary offerings.

Jesus does mention the tithe when reprimanding the pharisees (Matthew 23:23; Luke 11:42), but it was used sarcastically and we must remember that, until the Cross, Israel was still operating under the Old Covenant and the complete Law of Moses. The Temple was still in operation and the feasts and festivals were still observed.

The Apostle Paul says in 2 Corinthians 9:6–8, **"Now this *I say*, he who sows sparingly will also reap sparingly, and he who sows bountifully will also reap bountifully. Each one *must do* as he has purposed in his heart, not grudgingly or under compulsion, for God loves a cheerful giver. And God is able to make all grace abound to you, so that always having all sufficiency in everything, you may have an abundance for every good deed."**

Besides generously and cheerfully as admonished above, Paul also writes of giving sacrificially, regularly, and proportionally. And while giving proportionally could fit in with everyone giving 10%, Paul does not suggest the tithe or any other specific percentage.

Personally (not meant for you to adopt or mimic), I use 10% as a means to measure where I am with my giving. I do not necessarily calculate out a tithe with each offering check I write, but whether it was my upbringing in a church that preached the tithe or a personal conviction, I always try to give at least 10%, but usually more. There has also been some trying times when 10% was not possible. God abundantly blessed in each season of my life because He knows my heart and my desire in giving.

Whether you believe in a mandated tithe or something else, just make sure it is based on your conviction from the Scripture under the covenant or grace, and not under a legalistic mandate. Also, your offering should not be the same as paying the electric bill, meaning it should not be so regimented and automatic that you give no thought or prayer as to what God would have you to give. Don't turn an act of worship into the mindless writing of a check.

Getting back to our Proverb brings us back to understanding that we have been taught the wrong math, and the wrong ideas. When we live our lives according to the world's math, we miss out on the blessings of depending upon God and allowing Him the joy of providing everything we will ever need. When we skip out on honoring God with our giving first, and instead look at what's leftover before determining what our offerings will be, we are depending on human logic which also circumvents the blessings reserved for us.

If, at this time, you find yourself in a deep hole from ignoring God's principles or not taking them seriously enough, you have some work to do before being able to give as you probably would like to. So, get busy, because our view of handling of money is often a spotlight on certain areas of our lives.

Does money change a person's character, or does it bring a person's true character to the surface? I propose that the latter is closer to the truth of the matter. I do not think that money changes a person at all. I believe the character that lies within them is simply magnified when money is in great supply. People who are generous when they are poor remain generous when they have more money. Those who do not spread their money around when they have little will not spread it around if they have more.

Through the years, I have had many folks in the various churches I have been a part of tell me about all the great things they would do if God would let them win the lottery. There are so many things wrong with that statement, I cannot begin to list them all—but let's just say for a moment that I agree it's okay to play the lottery (which I don't). If they are not contributing to the church with their offerings now, I guarantee they would not give much even if they did win the lottery. Changing your character will not happen simply because your bank account has changed. Those who chase the dollar will put their trust in the dollar, and thus having more dollars will not affect their generosity toward the church or their fellow man.

One of the pitfalls of trusting in money is the attitude you will have toward those who do not have much of it. **"The poor man utters supplications, but the rich man answers roughly"** (18:23).

The poor of this world are, in many ways, dependent upon the wealthy. Their means of providing for themselves are limited and often times need help and assistance from others just to keep food on the table and a roof over their heads. And, while there are some who are simply lazy and refuse to work, there are others who do everything within their power to provide for themselves and their families—they simply cannot accomplish the task on their own. So, why is it that so many look down on the legitimately needy?

I have never been poor, but I have been in positions where I have needed a handout. It is a humiliating position to be in—especially when you finally come to the point of asking for help. As humiliating as that is, it is even worse when the person you go to refuses to help or places conditions on helping you. Now, there are times when accountability definitely needs to be put in place, but I am talking about having an attitude of superiority and using your "elevated" position to beat a person down a little further.

God's Word is clear that we are to lend generously when asked and we are to be very careful about borrowing. There is nothing that reveals your level of godliness more so than how you use money. Treating the money God provides you with as your own reveals an attitude of trusting in that money. Treating the money God provides to you as His reveals an attitude of trusting in God.

So, what is your attitude about money, especially in giving it away? A good test is in how generous you are. If you are giving to the church as God outlines in His Word and you are giving to those who are needier than you, then you most likely have a proper attitude toward money. God will continue to provide for your needs as He has promised. If your giving is sporadic or nonexistent, then your attitude toward money is unbiblical and the dollar will be your god. Either way, your character will be on display for all to see regardless of the amount you possess.

One other test: if these words bothered you or made you angry with me …

* * *

There are many kinds of laws in our world; the law of gravity is the easiest to illustrate. This law is in effect whether or not you believe it or understand it. If you go up on your roof and step off, you will fall to the ground—hard! You can't go up to the roof and say you don't believe in gravity and thus will not fall—well, I guess you could say it, but you're still going to fall. The other laws of physics are just as certain, as well as many other physical laws God created.

There is another set of laws that are also just as certain. Many refer to them as moral laws, but we should simply call them God's laws. The laws God records for us in His Word are sure and certain (they aren't called the Ten Suggestions). And while the Ten Commandments are better known, they are simply a summation of the many other laws of God. If you break one of these laws, you will suffer the accompanying consequence—in God's timing, and that's the key. We may not suffer the same immediate consequence of stepping off our roof, but we will suffer the consequence nonetheless at some point in the future.

Here's an example of one of God's laws—**"He who shuts his ear to the cry of the poor will also cry himself and not be answered"** (21:13).

We sometimes refer to this law as, "What goes around, comes around" or one of any number of other quaint sayings, but it is simply God's law of sowing and reaping (Galatians 6:7). Solomon applies this law to our treatment of those who are in need. If we ignore the people who are truly in need (not those who choose to not work when they are capable), then we, too, will be ignored when we have a need.

So, how far do we take this? Does this law apply to every person you pass by on the street corners and exit ramps holding up a sign? No, but if you open your heart to the Holy Spirit's leading, He will help; and we need His divine discernment.

While this law of God deals with anyone who has a need that you have the ability to fill, I believe the primary application deals with those in your sphere of influence; those in your community, your family, your church, etc. If you are willing to be a servant to the Lord, He will make it extremely clear to you when you are to help someone else with your time, your talent, and your treasure—and that will pretty much be those whose needs are made known to you when you have the means to assist.

Your generosity will, in turn, be visited upon you, and your indifference will, in turn, be visited upon you. It is a law of God and it is always in effect—just like gravity. If your generosity is abused or you get taken advantage of, God will handle things on both sides—so let Him!

Most people of us struggle to maintain a generous attitude and spirit. Some want no part of it and others simply are much too controlled by his or her own fleshly desires. And then there are some who are generous with their money but are stingy with their time, or vice versa. Generosity is measured in many aspects of our lives—not just the ease in which we part with "our" money.

"He who is generous will be blessed, for he gives some of his food to the poor" (22:9).

Solomon's primary point is clearly how we share the financial resources God entrusts to our care—and let me say right up front, every penny you have in your possession and every material good you own has been provided for you by God. He is the One who gives you the health to be able to earn an income, He is the One who has given you a functioning brain, and He is the One who even ordained that you be born in a country that affords you the opportunity to accumulate wealth. Apart from God's provision, you would have absolutely nothing.

After supplying all these things, God then allows us the freedom to hoard or distribute. We can continue to buy nicer and newer stuff, or we can be content and look for opportunities to share. We can accumulate treasures here on earth that will eventually deteriorate, or we can accumulate treasure in heaven that will last for eternity. We can appease the fleshly desire to have more or we can submit to the Father's will by resisting the flesh.

Solomon says we are **blessed** when we handle God's money with a generous spirit. God uses our generosity to provide **food to the poor**—and the lesson in this is vitally important in understanding the heart of God. God sees the need of the poor and He hears their cries, but He chooses to fill these needs by also filling a hidden need we are usually not even aware of. Those of us who have means to share with others (and we all have something to share) have a tremendous need for godly contentment. And when we follow God's principle of generosity, God fills the need for contentment in our lives while filling the needs of those who are hungry. Giving displays contentment with God's provision.

Allow me to share another principle we find in the Book of Acts. **"And the congregation of those who believed were of one heart and soul; and not one *of them* claimed that anything belonging to him was his own, but all things were common property to them. And with great power the apostles were giving testimony to the resurrection of the Lord Jesus, and abundant grace was upon them all. For there was** not a needy person among them, for all who were owners of lands and houses would sell them and bring the proceeds of the sales and lay them at the apostles' feet, and they would be distributed to each as any had need" (Acts 4:32–35).

While we are probably familiar with this story, I believe most Christians miss an important principle related to us here—the people sold some of their possessions to meet the needs of the others. They didn't write a check or reach into their pocket, but instead they sold something they owned to meet the need. I am convinced that, if we would practice this same example given here to us in God's Word, the grip that money and possessions has over us would be loosened. For when you sell a possession, you are letting go and proving they are not truly yours to keep. Until our money has been used to purchase something, it typically does not have the same power over us. Once the purchase has been made, the sense of ownership takes over to a greater extent.

I once read a book by a godly author who branded this principle in my mind with his attitude and actions. He did not view anything he possessed as his own and related several personal examples of this attitude—including giving away his car to someone who had need as the Holy Spirit prompted him. His prayer was something to the effect of, *"This car belongs to You, Lord, what would you have me to do?"*

One of the Wesley brothers was once told that his house had burned to the ground. His reply was along the lines of, the house belonged to God and it was now one less thing for him to be concerned with.

I have since tried to apply this principle when issues of finance and possessions could cause me pain and worry. One particular instance of note involved a tax problem. Unbeknownst to my wife and I, our tax preparer had been unknowingly filing our taxes improperly. The result was we owed over $35,000 in taxes, interest, and penalties. My prayer was immediately, *"God, You owe the IRS $35,000, how would You like me to proceed?"*

We had some savings, so we emptied that to pay what we could, but it was only a portion. We then went through the process to set up a payment plan, which meant seven years of indebtedness. The very day I sent in the paperwork, I received a call from someone who knew of our situation. He said that he and his wife wanted to help. I thought that meant a small contribution to the amount owed, but he then told me that I didn't understand their offer—they wanted to pay the entire balance! I almost dropped the phone and I choked up at their generosity and how God once again provided!

Everything belongs to God. When we operate under this truth, and I mean truly operate under this truth, prepare yourself for the amazing and the miraculous provision of the Lord. Don't miss what I wrote previously about being sure to follow all of His precepts and principles, but, when we do and when we attribute that all belongs to Him, get ready!

* * *

TAKE ACTION

Handling money is the most neglected of life skills. You can go through grade school, high school, and get multiple university degrees without ever being taught anything about handling money or balancing a checkbook. Yet, God spends more time discussing money in His Word than any other topic except possibly relationships. So, again, accept that you are likely deficient in your understanding on this essential topic, and lacking in the necessary skills.

Now that you have read through the principles given here, consider starting over with pen and paper by your side. Start writing down each issue you need help with, each action you need to take, and each habit you need to start.

God never intended for money to be a burden. He has clearly given us the blueprint for tremendous success and joy—and it is available to everyone at any stage of your life, no matter how poorly you have handled things thus far. You can start right now. The journey may be long and difficult, but the destination is more than worth the effort. His incredible blessings await!

Grace and peace to you!